IS

FOR REAL:

How to build the best relationship and
get the most out of your vet
so your pet wins!
Finally, the secrets revealed.

By

Dr Lennon Foo

BVetMed GPCert(SAM) MRCVS

Copyright © DR LENNON FOO 2020

This book is sold subject to the condition that it shall not, by way of trade or otherwise, be lent, resold, hired out, or otherwise circulated without the publisher's prior consent in any form of binding or cover other than that in which it is published and without a similar condition including this condition being imposed on the subsequent publisher.

The moral right of DR LENNON FOO has been asserted.

ISBN-13: 978-1-8381696-0-2

www.amityvets.co.uk

www.drlennonfoo.com

ismyvetforreal@gmail.com

For you, who embraced the immense responsibility and burden of pet guardianship.

For my beloved veterinary profession, providing my life's calling.

For the animals, which without them, the world would certainly be a much duller place.

Dear Chloe,

With Compliment,

Lennon Lue 2021

ADVANCE PRAISES

'The best way to show your pet you love them is to make sure they are healthy, and Dr. Foo's book will help you do just that. It's a must-read guide that answers your questions around veterinarians and your pet's healthcare.'
- Robin Farmanfarmaian, Professional speaker and Entrepreneur, Palo Alto, CA

*

'Funny, innovative and fantastic. Lennon has written an insightful guide that will enhance and empower any pet owner – A MUST READ!!!!!'
– Dr Luke Gamble FRCVS, CEO Worldwide Veterinary Service and Mission Rabies, New Forest, UK

*

'Dr Lennon Foo's wealth of experience and knowledge can only enhance our expectations and relationships. It is clearly evident from his book that he is an advocate for the human-animal bond. The book demonstrates his deep compassion both for animals and for the human side of the equation, along with a nice sprinkling of humour. Lennon also offers insight into the importance of emotional well-being, enrichment, and the

reduction of fear, anxiety, and stress in our pets.

As a dog guardian the book has provided me with a greater understanding of my Vet and how we can work together to ensure my dogs needs and that my expectations are managed.

As a practising canine behaviourist, the book has given me a deeper insight to the Veterinary side of behaviour consults and how valuable it is to ensure we work in partnership with the dogs vet.'

- Lisa Hird, Head Behaviourist Canine Behaviour College/Animal Courses Direct
Vice Chair INTO Dogs, Lincolnshire, UK

*

'This informative and insightful book is a must-read for every pet guardian. Dr. Lennon Foo explains clearly and eloquently how to foster mutual understanding and harmony with your veterinarian, and demonstrates why this will have a hugely beneficial impact on both you and your pet companion.'

- Lisa Tenzin-Dolma, Founder and Principal of The International School for Canine Psychology & Behaviour Ltd., Bath, England

*

'I was hooked from the first paragraph and couldn't put it down. This guide is written in an entertaining manner whilst delivering practical and straight-forward advice. A great insight into the life of a vet and all it entails, both good and bad, whilst providing you with the knowledge and confidence

to speak to your vet without fear, about your pet's medical needs.'

- Caroline Gale (IMDT), Dog Trainer,
Newton Abbot, UK

*

'This book is a must have for all pet owners, regardless of species! In this book Lennon provides the essential 'know-how' you need to work as your pet's guardian and form a lasting relationship with them and your vet'.

– Denise O'Moore,
Chair Association of IntoDogs, UK

*

'This book is a must for all Pet Owners. Easy to read, very interesting, practical and full of helpful tips and information. Dr Lennon Foo, is a REAL great Vet! He has always provided us with the best care for our pet and filled us with nothing but confidence.'

- Katrina Oliver (Community Care Worker) & Brad Oliver (Professional Ice Skater), Chudleigh, UK

*

'A vet actively encouraging you to ask questions and to be part of the whole process, in the treatment of your pet. A refreshing read, a must for all vets and guardians alike.'

– Jenn Whitehorn, Dog Walker, UK

*

'Lennon is the most genuine, kind, loving and knowledgeable vet I have ever known and it is a great privilege to work with him. He really understands the importance of the interaction between vet, animal and guardian. This is a wonderful and long awaited book that all pet Guardians need to read.'

- Shimara Hawkins, Author and Healer,
South Brent, UK

*

'Every pet owner should read Dr Lennon's book to realise the importance of communication between themselves and their vet. Every vet in training should also read to realise that being an exceptional vet is medical knowledge AND understanding human emotions.'

- Sue Bowers, Newton Abbot, Devon, UK

*

'I have learned things that I never knew before and feel empowered to make sure my pet's medical needs are sorted and are aligned with my beliefs and expectations.'

- Carol Simmons, Retired teacher,
Newton Abbot, UK

*

'I have been with Amity for several years now as I have always found that Lennon and his team treat you as being as important as your pet; that visiting

this veterinary practice is so different from ones that I previously used for decades before joining Amity. This new book shows you the reader how important that you are as the carer for your pet, and that being understood is as important as the care that your pet receives; buying this book will give you the confidence in dealing with your vet, what you should expect and how to achieve this.'

— Jeston Brightmore-Armour,
retired, Christow, UK

*

'This guide delivers the most practical and straightforward tutorial I have ever read and in these sad times (of COVID 19) it made me smile at the end. Well done, Lennon.'

- Tessa Henley, B&B Owner, Dawlish, UK

*

'From the very first visit to Lennon Foo's at Amity Vets we knew this was how a vet's practice should be and this book reinforces that view whilst giving an insight to his unique approach.'

- Karel & Mona Moudry, retired,   Exmouth, UK

*

'In the time I have come to know Lennon and his assistants, my visits to his practice have been made easy and far less painful, from the vets I have used before, Lennon treats all his pet owners and pets with lots of love and affection and he will never

judge you, you can ask him for his advice and you will get the answer you want. Amity Vets are there for you at all times and if you have an animal you want register than go and see Lennon and his staff.'
- Andrew Norris, Carer, Devon, UK

*

'I now possess the knowledge to be my pet's hero and guardian and can speak to my vet with confidence.'
- Sara Casadei Gardini, Assistant Restaurant Manager, Newton Abbot, UK

*

'More please! A brilliant read. Enlightening, honest and funny. A must for all 'animal guardians'. A different approach from a wonderfully different man and his dedicated team.'
- Julia Hill, Illustrator, Devon, UK

CONTENTS

ACKNOWLEDGEMENTS

I have to start by thanking my beautiful wife, Fanny Amity whose name inspired a pet guardian-centric vet practice and whose patience allowed this book to be written. Writing my first book is one of the most difficult and daunting things I have done. Thank you for giving me space to do so. This book would not be possible without your support. Thank you so much, my gentle love.

I will be eternally grateful to my parents aka Mummy and Papa. Allowing me to breathe in this world with independence and supporting the way I choose to live with no judgement or prejudice is more than I can ever ask. Without your help, I would not even be a vet in the first place. Thank you and I love you so much.

Reminding me daily about the importance of keeping the inner child in me alive, I would like to thank my sons, Devon and Toren. You keep me young and playful. Thank you for showing me how to look at the wondrous world through innocent eyes again. You are a great teacher of simple and profound gratitude. You are proof that age is just a number and everyone has a lesson to teach. Thank you for reminding how limitless our genius and powers can be. Thank you for showing me how to live.

My amazing sister, Shennon, who provided a sense of belonging for me all these years abroad. You have taken care of me more than I have done so for you and for that, I am grateful you are my blood.

Dr Josephine Tan, the first vet I have ever worked for and introduced me to veterinary medicine. Your compassion for animals and their guardians have paved a starting point for my dream and career. Your patience and knowledge have inspired me to remain humble and hungry to learn. Thank you so much for your teachings and taking me under your wings twenty years ago. I cannot stop here not mentioning the team I worked with, Cheryl Siow, Adam and Audrey Tan, we had crazy times! Frankel Pets Clinic will always be a special place for me.

Special thanks to Wei Tjia kor kor for being as strong a support now as you were more than 25 years ago. You have watched me grow up and I have been lucky to have you as family. Thank you for believing in me and my journey.

Also to Uncle Han Cheong (Jigu) who believed and invested in me not too long ago. Thank you and I will show you that you have great investment acumen.

Never forgetting Uncle Andrew Cheng, Ong Lay Hong (Qiyi) and Kuang who also saw the potential in me. Thank you and you ROCK as a family!

Through the ups and downs of the last two decades of

my life, Carol and Martin King, you have been there for me. A solid rock that I never expected in a foreign land. Somehow, you always saw the good in me. Thank you for taking care of me, celebrating my successes and supporting me through my tribulations.

I feel luckier than Charlie for I have not three but four Angels in my life. Despite thousands of miles separating us, we nurtured and invested in our friendship, resulting in something special and timeless. Thank you Beatrice Yuen, Linda Lim, Lynette Koh and Adeline Sim for our laughter, tears and joy for nearly three decades. I am truly blessed.

No man is an island. I would not be able to do what I do without my fantastic Amity Team. They are the most incredible group of people I know. One, for doing what they do and two, for putting up with me. Thank you for allowing me to lead you and teaching me daily, especially Ella Woodfield.

The world is a better place thanks to people who want to develop and lead others. What makes it even better are people who share the gift of their time to mentor future leaders. Thank you COL Oh Beng Soon (retired) who showed me the possibility of being a great boss while running around the jungle more than twenty years ago.

Thank you Andrew Hale for writing the foreword and Neil Thomas (Animal In Distress) for providing the facts and figures. You ROCK!

Special thanks to Princess Robin Starbuck Soloway Farmanfarmaian for inspiring the chapter '**Don't tell me what to do with my pet!** The Pet Guardian as CEO: You are in Charge!' I am struck in awe by your humbleness despite your great success. You deserve every bit of good in the world. You are royalty with or without your title and a complete inspiration to the medical field! Thank you for your energy and positivity. You are pure dynamite!

Exceptional gratitude must be extended to Karen Gidley, who watched me grow in my entire career and always believing in me. You brought nobility to the profession and an inspiration to me that amazing practice managers do exist. You demonstrated extreme patience and perseverance in my early years which I will always be grateful for.

Thank you, Dan 'The Man' Lok. Your teachings have reinforced and validated my views I felt about life. I make no excuses, harbour no opinions and certainly am no victim. #HTCforlife

I would also like to thank Tucker Max from Scribe and the Scribe Method. Without which, there is NO WAY this book could have been written. The work you are doing is so important. Keep it up!!

Special thanks to William and Susanna Wicks for your ever enduring support!

Last but not least, a very special thanks to Amity members especially Val Doderer, Margaret and Keith

Butler, Jeston Brightmore-Armour, Mona with Karel Moudry, Sue Bowers and Bats Batten with Faye Brereton who contributed their stories of their pets. Also to Diane Inci, Jon Cleave, Jayne Baker, Lauren Bassett and Josh Sword, Milena Sokowska, Sara Casedei Gardini and Martin Woodcock, Donna Kerr, Tracey Howitt, Liz Palethrope, Pat and Norman Hutton, Holly King and Holly Parmenter, Yvette and Molly Mitchell, Charlotte Mills, Ann Lancaster, Delsi May Watkins, Shelley and John Clifton, Martin and Terry Allen, Denise Barton, Chris and Kelly Edgecombe, Chris Linnitt, Megan Johnson, Amy Robinson, Carol Sinclair-Day, Shimara Hawkins, Sian Day, OJ and Andy Gillson and Andrew Norris for allowing me to make a living doing what I love and not feeling like I am working! What a rush! You have my deepest gratitude. Thank you.

FOREWORD

Traditionally there has been a measure of suspicion between owners of companion animals and the veterinary professionals they employ to support them. This can be based on anything from the perception of excessive charges to the delivery of a poor bedside manner. Equally, some vets have not always had the easiest of times with some clients, with often a breakdown of communication underlying many of those challenges. All in all, historically, the relationship between owner and vet has not always been the most positive.

As a Certified Animal Behaviourist, I work closely with the veterinary team to ensure best outcomes for the animals I am helping. One thing I have learned in many years of collaboration with vets is that not all vets are the same! The culture of the vet practices and the individual personality of the clinician are important variables in how easy a working relationship can be found. I also know how difficult it can be for those best outcomes when the relationship between the clinical team and the owner starts to break down.

Dr Lennon Foo has identified the importance of that culture and personality, and I know first-hand how he believes in, and promotes, a client-centred, supportive approach. Changing culture has always been his focus, and through his Amity brand he is successfully changing how owners see their vet experience.

'Is My Vet For Real' represents an important step forward in bridging the gap between vet and owner. It helps empower the animal's carer by educating them in the structure and practice of the veterinary system. Importantly it affords them a glimpse into the mind of many vets, as well as a better understanding of the pressures and responsibilities they experience daily. He has cleverly lifted the veil that often lies between vet and owner, dispelling many of the myths and misunderstandings that can hamper good working relationships.

As well as dealing with many aspects of the dynamic between the vet and her client, Lennon also cleverly examines the psychology that underpins it. He has a wonderful philosophy to life, love and our sense of self and this shines through the text as you read through. There is much to be learnt from this book beyond just our relationship with our vets.

Lennon has a great gift in communicating important, sometimes complex, topics and concepts in an understandable and interesting way. He has a fun and engaging style which makes reading this book not only informative but really enjoyable. The only question I have is, why hasn't a book like this been written before now? It really is much needed, and I hope many pet owners and vets get to read it.

- *Andrew Hale, BSc Certified Animal Behaviourist*

LET'S START FROM

THE VERY BEGINNING

A Vet's Confession

Treating animals is only half my job. It takes half my time, half my energy and half my attention. Which may sound nothing short of dangerous for your pet!! But this actually makes me a VERY good vet. Because the other half of my attention is on you, the human being, in the middle, the "Pet Guardian". YOU are the person who lives with, loves and knows the story of your wonderful animal companion.

Unfortunately, most people have poor experiences with vets, which can lead to bad outcomes, which is really sad. If you are struggling to get your vet to listen, and you know you aren't getting the results that your pet needs and deserves, IT IS NOT YOUR FAULT, and I'm here to tell you that you are not alone. I think we need to repeat that, IT IS NOT YOUR FAULT.

I have been a successful vet for more than 15 years, and I can tell you that there is a better way for both your pet and you...

Anna is the pet guardian of Tinker, a fit and well Springer Spaniel on a "raw food" diet. But her vet didn't know. She was worried every time she saw her vet that they would find out. She knew it was best for her pet and she hated lying, but she felt afraid. She thought her vet would blame the diet for her dog's illnesses. She knew he was better on the diet, but she was so afraid that she used to make up the name of a dry dog food. The problem was, she couldn't remember the name of the food and always came up with a new name at reception. She gained a reputation as someone who constantly changed her dog's diet and, of course her vet thought that may be contributing to poor Tinker's illness!

Sally is another pet guardian who hates going to her vet. Her dog, Brutus, a lively Bull Terrier, gets very stressed in the busy waiting area. Sally gets embarrassed and was always afraid that she would be told off, so she said nothing and suffered in silence. She takes the dog in for treatment less and less and avoids talking to the vet team. This means Brutus isn't receiving the best treatment.

Mark took his cat, Milo, to the vet because he was constantly licking nasty bald patches and causing scabs. It was in a very sorry state but his vets would not listen. Every time he went, a new vet told him it was a flea allergy. His vets didn't believe that Mark was treating the fleas enough and used to say, 'Well, it just takes one flea.' They didn't listen when Mark pointed out that he ran a cattery and had some experience. It took 18 months to get the right diagnosis (food allergy was diagnosed in the end) and Milo suffered horribly. Milo's guardians did too; every time his wife looked at poor Milo, she was almost in tears. She knew it was cruel. If only their vets had listened...

Do you moan about your vet, about the pricing, about how they do not listen? Do you get frustrated about communication (or lack of)? Do you feel rushed, ignored, patronised and disappointed? You might feel like your vet misunderstood you and you were certainly not in control of the situation. Did you sometimes feel helpless and without a choice? Perhaps you felt stupid (not intentionally) and confused. Perhaps your expectations were not met by reality. Sometimes, unexplained rage or fear may occur without knowing why. It is so sad to see you suffer when in reality, you only want the best for your pet.

IT DOESN'T HAVE TO BE LIKE THIS!

Imagine all your concerns, expectations and feelings being heard, accepted and appreciated. What if your vet asks how *you* have been affected by your pet's illness? Imagine having no prejudice or fear when you are helping your pet to recover. You are not just a pet guardian who only sees the vet when your pet is unwell.

You are a unique individual, filled with dreams, expectations and fears, just like anyone else. You are certainly not someone that needs to be told what to do with your pet. You should be the one in charge and feel in control at all times about your beloved pet. What if your vet appreciates and values your help when diagnosing and treating your pet? Imagine getting excited to see your vet knowing that together, you will find the most appropriate treatment for your pet because not only does she know how to make your pet better (which is essential!), she also knows how to make you feel better (which is crucial!) to allow both your pet and you to win. Caring for your pet in this way can even be good for your mental health. What would that mean to you?

I am going to show you precisely how to do this. I am going to pull back the curtains that shroud veterinary medicine and help you to understand how your vet thinks. I will also show you step by step how to achieve the best relationship you can with your vet. You will be armed with knowledge that allows you to be your pet's hero and play an active role in helping your pet get better from illnesses. You will be shown trade secrets (like your vet's biggest fears) to allow you to understand, empathise and build a meaningful relationship with her. You will be empowered with simple facts and truths that will improve your confidence and faith that you are your pet's CEO and you stay in charge always. I'll walk you through step by step until you have mastered everything necessary to get your results.

Be sure to highlight bits that resonate, underline useful pointers and dog-ear (excuse the pun!) relevant pages. *Use* the book, don't just *read* it.

Before I became a vet, I was already a pet guardian, like you. I remember taking my seven-year-old female black and tan Miniature Pinscher, Miu miu, to the vets because she was unwell. I was incredibly stressed because I did not know if it was something that I did and just felt guilty for not being able to keep her healthy. When I brought her to my vet, I felt she did not listen to me and just wanted to give multiple injections and oral medication to my dog. Following that, further testing had to be performed as Miu miu was not getting better. I saw a different vet and received slightly different advice. I did not feel supported as I felt the communication was not enough to allow my understanding. Eventually, Miu miu got better and I changed vets after that. I knew there had to be a better way. Going to the vets cannot be this hard.

When I graduated from the Royal Veterinary College, I realised that while I was armed with more knowledge about animals than I had ever expected, I did not learn much about you, the wonderful pet guardian. The entire degree focused mainly on how to find out what is wrong and how to treat your pet. I started Amity Vets whose core purpose is to Empower You Through Education as I believe veterinary medicine should extend further than merely treating animals. It should also include and embrace the unique beauty of the bond between your pet and you. I have had the privilege and honour to work with over 10,000 pet guardians, performed over 60,000 consultations and had more than 90,000 pet guardian interactions. I have had good days and bad days. I have performed consultations that I wished I had done better and others that have changed lives. I speak humbly when I say I have learnt more from pet guardians than I have taught them.

Focusing on pet guardians as much as their pets has brought astounding results to all. They were happier, I felt my job was more meaningful and their pets benefitted the most. I started helping other pet guardians (who were seeing other vets) and they achieved the same results. I found out that this can be accomplished for any pet guardian, including you. Many of them have urged me to share this knowledge and insight. I felt compelled to write this book to do just that. I believe there is so much more goodwill your vet can bring to you that extends further than merely treating your pets.

If you have a great relationship with your vet, this book

will help to enhance it. If you have not and wish to, this book will give you a solid foundation to build upon.

This book does not, however, guarantee that your vet will work with you. Just like all pet guardians are different and unique, not all vets are the same. Just like how you would choose who to make friends with, you should be choosing a vet that suits you. Sometimes it is just a bad fit. This book will provide you the best insights to recognise the fit (or not) and develop a mutual understanding and respect with your vet.

(Considering there are more female vets than male vets at present, to avoid confusion and to keep it simple, I have referred vets as female and pets as male.)

To start, let's take a look at the very basis of veterinary medicine. What and who is it for? Does it impact your pet or you more?

UNTIL YOU HAVE LOVED AN ANIMAL, A PART OF YOUR SOUL REMAINS UNAWAKENED.

– Anatole France.

MY PET HATES HIS VET

BUT I THINK SHE IS SWELL!

Is Veterinary Medicine Impacting

Your Pet or You?

I remember treating a feisty cat that did not like to be handled. He had to be wrapped in a towel like a cat burrito for me to examine the burst abscess near his face (typically, it would be close to the mouth where sharp teeth are!). It was draining well and was fairly clean, thus only needed antibiotics and pain relief. He was snarling all this time and I wasn't convinced that he felt like I was helping him at all. I am not convinced that there was any love for my involvement or gratitude for my help. On the other hand, his owner was extremely relieved with the outcome, learning it was just an infection that would resolve soon with medication. At this moment in time, I wondered if my skills and capacity as a vet were impacting the pet guardian or her pet more. Does veterinary medicine actually help the animals more than their guardians? I think it is quite the opposite.

In this chapter, we will discuss how veterinary medicine has impacted both animal and human welfare. We will also discuss whether the animals or their human guardians get more out of the profession.

- **Veterinary Medicine is…**

Veterinary Medicine is defined as the **science** and **art** that deals with the maintenance of health and the prevention, alleviation, cure of disease and injury in animals and especially domestic animals. (Merriam-Webster Dictionary)

It is easy and straightforward to see how veterinary medicine can be a science. However, how is it an art? Art is the expression or application of human creative skill and imagination, typically in a visual form such as painting or sculpture, producing works to be appreciated primarily for their beauty or emotional power. How does it apply to veterinary medicine?

Veterinary medicine can be more than a science, dealing primarily with hard facts, pristine analysis, calculated risks and compelling evidence. As defined above, it is also an expression of imagination producing works to be appreciated for the emotional power that comes with it. There is much more goodwill to be produced than merely getting the animal better. Learning the science of veterinary medicine without the art is only doing half the job.

Very simply, your vet helps you to keep your pet healthy by advising you. For example, suggestions that involve your pet's environment, nutrition, and lifestyle could be made. She may also help manage the emotional aspect of your pet. If your pet is not well, she will find out what is wrong and offer treatment to regain his health or manage his condition.

When I was a child, I remember going to my vet and feeling mystified about what vets do. It was almost like magic. She asks a few questions, looks over my dog for a few minutes, gives me some tablets and miraculously, my dog is well again. It is no wonder that vets have been described as animal magicians.

Over the years of practising, many pet guardians have commented that it must be cool to be a vet. We get to treat animals and do cool things. Some are surprised at what we do and the knowledge that we have. In reality, not many people outside the industry really know what vets do, except that they help to get animals better.

• **How does your vet help you?**

The simple answer would be that your vet makes your pet feel better. Whether it is giving medicine, performing a surgery or even euthanasia, it is usually done to improve the situation. Many times, advice may be given to allow understanding of your pet's condition or prevent future episodes from recurring.

Sometimes the value given does not stop there. It may include a bit of counselling; an example would be if you felt it was your fault (when it wasn't) that your pet was ill. The feeling of guilt can be strong and you may take it harder than needed, causing a detrimental outcome. Or grief counselling after euthanasia. It is not unusual for you to feel depressed after a long period of time and you may speak often to your vet because of it.

When I was six months qualified, I was helping a three-year-old Shih Tzu called Pickles get over a skin infection. When he had gotten better and it was the last consultation for the all-clear sign-off, his guardian not only paid the consultation but also gave me a thank you card with £10 slipped into it. It was then I realised that the amount of goodwill I created for this pet guardian extended beyond the health of her pet I was treating.

My colleague reported that her client had willed a painting worth thousands of pounds to her for taking care of her and her Doberman. That was truly a humbling and grateful moment I felt about being a vet.

Around the world, there are about 1.8 million vets. The most important one is your vet.

- **I love being a vet**

In UK, there are more than 20,000 vets and over 5,000 vet practices.

As a profession, it does have its challenges and its benefits.

Due to the high number of vets quitting, veterinary surgeons have been placed on the Job Shortage List. It has been estimated that 10% of recent vet graduates want to leave the profession and up to 50% of them feel that their career has only met some of the expectations or not met any at all.

In addition, a vet in the UK is twice as likely to commit suicide compared to the medical field and four times more likely to do so compare to the general public.

However, practising veterinary medicine in the UK (compared to most of the other countries) does benefit from several factors.

Its benefits include the social attitude from the British where pets are more often seen as companions and/or family members than an accessory, unlike many other countries. It allows a higher level of veterinary medicine to be performed as the pet guardians are more interested and motivated. This permits greater satisfaction for you, your vet and of course, your pet. I have worked in countries where the public awareness is not as high and veterinary work is very different. There are usually more neglect cases than true medical issues.

For example, when I was working in Singapore, there were plenty of 'rubber band' cases. This is when someone had placed a rubber band around their pet's head and neck to hold his ears up so they do not go into the food bowl during feeding. It sounds incredible but it is true. Unfortunately, the problem begins when they forget to remove the rubber band... sometimes for days. The rubber band then stops blood circulation and cuts into the skin of the dog, causing trauma, infection, swelling, flesh dying and pain. It is a situation arisen from ignorance and neglect, not disease. Thankfully, I have not seen this in the UK.

Greater demand for advanced techniques and specialism from pet guardians has allowed many vets to pursue their chosen field of interest to learn more and deliver more. This does come at a price. Increased specialism, equipment and facilities cost more. The cost of the service is usually higher because of the extra time, effort and money put in to achieve that higher certification or status. Pet insurance has proved to be invaluable and essential. If there was no pet insurance, I am not sure if the advancements would have come as far and many referral centres could remain open.

The strong positive public support of the veterinary profession makes it better to be a vet in this country than several other countries. However, further improvements can be made to the relationship between the profession and the public. There is certainly more goodwill that can be provided and more value to be brought to all. What is needed is a slight shift in mindset.

I love vetting and feel it is one of the most incredible and satisfying job that ever existed! Where else can you find dinner conversations revolving around pus and sticking your hand in places where the sun doesn't shine (for a good cause, of course!)!

- **Vetting beyond treating animals**

There is a common factor linking all the animals being treated in the past and for the foreseeable future. All of them have a human guardian.

If your vet's job is to solely treat your pet's condition, she is placing a self-limiting belief in the opportunity given to her as a vet and reducing the amount of goodwill she could actually provide. She has been placed in a very unique and sacred position where she is able to influence your feelings not by what she does but how she does it.

Being by your side, giving you confidence and validation that what you are doing is correct, encouraging you to medicate and follow the instructions to get your pet better, commending you for taking on the responsibility of pet guardianship, are jobs that your vet need not do but it is critically important that she does them. These messages can be extremely powerful and meaningful coming from a place of authority. Likewise, any negative comment made can have profound effects on you.

As discussed in the story of the feisty cat above, I know that the impact on his pet guardian was so much more than treating him. So if your vet is purely interested only in your pet and derives satisfaction solely from helping him, not only is she going to be disappointed and dissatisfied as your pet may not express gratitude but more importantly, she has grossly limited the amount of goodwill she could potentially provide by not including you.

Trevor was an 18-year-old cat. He had advanced kidney failure and horrendous teeth that prevented him from eating properly. A dental procedure under general anaesthetic was desperately needed to improve his quality of life. This was what his guardian said: "My mother is 90 years old and has senile dementia. The only thing she can recognise in this world is Trevor. Please make sure he survives the general anaesthetic." When I heard that, I felt immense pressure to achieve the desired outcome. Not only was I treating this ancient cat with severe organ compromise, I was also given the responsibility of treating his guardian's ancient mum and affecting the outcome of family dynamics should I fail. Thankfully, in this particular case, Trevor survived his general anaesthetic, lived for another year with a healthy mouth and improved quality of life. His guardian's mother's relationship with Trevor did not deteriorate.

Treating your pet may be challenging. The diseases may vary in presentations and outcomes. However, treating you, especially your emotions, certainly poses a greater challenge. As it may be, it also results in greater satisfaction and sense of fulfilment.

Takeaway: Veterinary medicine has always been designed to impact your pet's life but inadvertently impact your life as well. Over time, its impact made on you seems to be greater than on your pet. The amount of goodwill given can be increased if your vet treats both your pet and you.

YOU TREAT A DISEASE, YOU WIN, YOU LOSE. YOU TREAT A PERSON, I GUARANTEE YOU, YOU'LL WIN, NO MATTER THE OUTCOME.

– Robin Williams in *Patch Adams*

Now that you understand more about veterinary medicine, it is time to find out about you, the wonderful pet guardian...

IS PET OWNERSHIP REAL OR

DO YOU ONLY THINK IT IS?

An Incredible Responsibility

and Burden

Did you know that in the UK (2018), it's estimated that incredibly, 12 million (44%) households have pets with around 51 million pets owned, of which 9 million are dogs and 8 million are cats? Unsurprisingly, over 88% of them say having a pet improves their quality of life. In the same year, a whopping £4.7 billion was spent on pet-related products and £5.2 billion was spent on veterinary bills and related services. The cost of owning a dog for its entire life in UK is about £6,500 to £17,000 depending on size and this does not include the vet bills!

Pet guardianship is a responsibility filled with immense physical, mental, financial and emotional demands. As many have described, it is like having a child. Vast amounts of time, effort and energy are expected and needed. You may have heard of pet guardians who have sacrificed travelling because of their pets. You may also know some friends who have cars specially fitted for their dogs. What about the couple that converted their home into a rehabilitation unit and dedicated their lives to saving wild birds that were brought in to them just for the chance that they might be released into the wild again? Perhaps you know someone like that. Maybe it is you.

In this chapter, we will explore pet guardianship. We will discuss the pros and cons and perhaps, why you chose to take on this responsibility. We will also discover whether pet guardianship is actually beneficial for the pet or not. We will then conclude with finding out how appropriate the term 'pet ownership' is.

- **This is why I got my pet!**

There are many reasons why having pets may be good for you. You know how much your furry (or non-furry) friend improves your quality of life. But it's not all about unconditional love – although that actually provides a wellness boost, too. On an emotional level, owning a pet can decrease depression, stress and anxiety. And health-wise, it can lower your blood pressure, improve your immunity and even decrease your risk of heart attack and stroke. But there is more...

In a 2002 study at State University of New York at Buffalo, researchers found that when conducting a stressful task, people experienced less stress when their pets were with them than when a spouse, family member or close friend was nearby. Don't tell the family!

While some studies have found a stronger connection than others, having a pet has the potential to lower blood pressure, especially in patients who have high blood pressure or are at risk.

Having a pet can reduce anxiety leading to reduction in pain, especially when his guardian is dealing with chronic pain like arthritis or migraines. Doris is a 75-year-old lady who claimed that her arthritis became worse when she was without her Tito, her beloved Yorkshire Terrier.

It improves your mood. It could be the unconditional love that they always exhibit, making you feel like a superstar and you never have to explain yourself on any occasion (unless you choose to!).

It helps you socialise. Owning a dog usually involves increased chances of meeting other people with a common interest. There is a similar effect when caring for any other pet. It creates a common bond with other pet guardians which may lead to increased interaction. In addition, an Austrian study "found that pet ownership led to an increase in social contact, more socialisation within neighbourhoods [such as neighbours chatting as they walk their dogs], and even a greater perception to observers that the neighbourhood seemed 'friendly.'" Also, it can keep the owners fitter from walking the dog!

Amazingly, it can prevent strokes and reduce heart attacks. It is believed that having a cat will reduce your chances of having a stroke by 30% and heart attack by 40%.

It can be used to monitor the blood sugar levels in diabetic patients. According to the American Diabetes Association's Diabetes Forecast magazine, a 1992 study found that one-third of the pets living with diabetics (mostly dogs, but other pets included cats, birds and rabbits) would change their behaviour when their guardian's blood sugar level dropped. Casper, a Yellow Labrador, would bark and look for his guardian whenever his 10-year-old son was starting to have a seizure episode.

In addition, it prevents allergies and increases immunity. Studies have shown that children who grew up on farms or around animals had lesser chance of getting allergies. The more pets you grew up with, the lesser the allergies.

Unsurprisingly, it helps children develop. Having a pet can allow your children to relate to others and allow them to express their feelings better.

You feel safer! If you are home alone, having a pet can make you feel safer. Also, burglars are less likely to target a house that is clearly a home to a dog (especially having a guard dog like a German Shepherd or simply any sized dog with a deep loud bark!).

All in all, the general feeling seems to be that having a pet creates positive emotions and is tremendously great for your health. But I suspect you already knew that!

- **If you can't take this, don't get a pet!**

So having a pet is not all fun and games, there are certainly obvious challenges involved as well.

It can certainly limit your movement. You may feel (rightfully or wrongfully) you are unable to leave your pet for extended periods of time so holidays may be sacrificed. You may also feel obliged or restricted that you can only go to pet (or dog) friendly places so it may limit the options of going out as well, e.g. going to the aquarium, certain restaurants. Pet guardians have mentioned that as a factor for not getting a new pet after their pet had passed away. Has your pet limited what you do?

It can cause stress and worry. Allowances have to be made for daily activities which could sometimes be undesirable, like a cat using your brand new leather couch as a scratching post or your puppy chewing your favourite snuggly slippers, expensive leather shoes or essential credit cards. Rob got extremely stressed because Bruce, his active Springer Spaniel, was being aggressive to other dogs on walks. He could not let Bruce, who loved free running, loose. He tried various training classes in vain. He was torn between rehoming his faithful companion, breaking his heart or persisting, breaking his will. Thankfully, with the right routine, Rob finally managed to crack the issue. But it did cause him extreme stress and worry for some time.

More thought has to be involved with having a live animal in your house. When they fall sick, it can cause immense worry and stress as well, before, during and after your vet visit. You may find it stressful getting your pet to your vet (you know how your cat 'loves' a car ride... not!), waiting in a busy reception area, learning about the illness and even coping with the treatment. Certainly, you may almost need to see your own doctor (and perhaps you do) due to the stress induced by your pet!

It can cause allergies. Sometimes, instead of improving the immune system or reducing allergies, the opposite can happen. Keep in mind that allergies can grow worse each time you are exposed to an allergen, so spending limited time with animals in the past is not conclusive proof you are not going to be allergic to them. If you're unsure of your animal allergies, pet sitting for a friend or spending time volunteering for an animal shelter might be something you want to try first. Have you got any pet-related allergies?

It can cause safety or health hazards. A pet might be a fabulous addition for your young family, however a large breed of dog, for example, will require extra attention and training to make sure it is safe around your children. Similarly, aggressive types of snakes or territorial pets may not be the best addition if you have young dependents living with you. If your pet is not toilet trained or has incontinence issues, it may not be suitable if you have a crawling young baby. Certainly, if you had an immunocompromised person living in your home, it would require more thought before obtaining a pet, or the choice of pet. Fundamentally, it is important to consider the needs of everyone in your home before getting a pet.

It can be costly. PDSA have estimated the average minimum costs for having a dog for its lifetime can range from £6,500 to £17,000, depending on size. This is the bare minimum cost. It may escalate to £33,000 if you decide or need to spend more in his ongoing care. Please bear in mind, this does NOT include the vet bills and that can certainly vary from hundreds to tens of thousands pounds depending on the condition and treatment. Pet insurance can help in these costs, especially relating to vet bills. It is also important to remember that not all costs are monetary; emotional costs like the stress induced and time spent are immeasurable.

It involves poop. It does not matter what pet you get, it will involve you clearing up after your pet in some way or another. Some poops are easier to clear than others. Be prepared for it and have a strong stomach if needed!

It can truly disrupt your life. Cats, for example, are naturally nocturnal, and are likely to find their way to be on top of you while you try to sleep. Similarly, dogs, birds, and many exotic animals will sometimes feel the need to make as much noise as possible in the middle of the night. Being prepared to take on these challenges when you decide it's time for a pet may ease your transition into pet guardianship much smoother. Donna, an avid pet guardian, had sacrificed her entire living room to her three dogs – a Weimaraner and two Spaniels. What have you sacrificed for your pet?

It is best to acknowledge, understand and accept the above before getting your pet. It may lead to better preparations, clearer expectations and greater joy when owning your pet.

- **My pet makes me feel amazing and tragic**

Having your pet can certainly elicit a wide range of emotions from you. You have heard the old adage, 'To you, he is just a dog. To him, you are everything.' As your pet's guardian, you are responsible for his emotional well-being. Whether he is happy, hungry, sad, anxious or excited, you are in control of it.

Perhaps, you were not aware of this responsibility and did not understand that it was indeed up to you to ensure your pet feels as safe, contented and happy as possible. Maybe you realise the responsibility only later and are not prepared to accept it and may feel it is more of a burden. On the other hand, you may have embraced the entire responsibility from the beginning and provided your best to support your pet emotionally.

Either way, it takes great courage, commitment, strength, love and conviction from you to take on the emotional responsibility of your pet.

A common positive feeling you may have is the feeling of achievement when your pet wanted for nothing and was as happy as could be under your care. The sense of satisfaction of providing a safe haven can be extremely gratifying. You can see it especially in young children when they feel responsible for their pet and know they have done a good job.

On the other hand, a common negative feeling you may have is the feeling of guilt when something happens to your pet. It may be when he goes missing, gets injured, falls sick or just simply, self-inflicted (i.e. nothing is wrong with the pet, you just think there is and feel guilty). Margaret always feels guilty thinking she has made her Chow-Chow dog, Timbo, fat by feeding too much and dreads weighing him at her vets even though he is in perfect body condition and of ideal weight! Or when Timbo falls ill and she feels guilty even though she has not done anything to bring about his illness. She just feels guilty because of the responsibility when caring for him.

It is also not uncommon for you to think it is your fault when your cat goes wandering away (and cats do!), thinking you have done something wrong to cause the wander. It really isn't the case!

As said, it is no mean feat taking on emotional responsibility like this. Most of the time, your pet does not really mind and is just grateful that he has you! Be kinder to yourself.

- **All I can think about it is... my pet!**

Having a pet can change the way you live your life. Depending on what sort of pet, the change could be extremely drastic (like having a dog) or minimal (like keeping a fish). Regardless, it certainly changes the way you think, plan and live your life.

If you have a pet, you will have to consider how your daily activities are going to affect him, being left on his own. This will impact how long you stay out for, how many hours you can work in a job that may not support working from home, how far you travel, extra provisions if you have to be away for an extended period of time like a holiday or for work. If you are able to take your pet with you, where can you go that is pet friendly or accommodating? Either way, it will certainly impact your choices and you will be conscious of your pet perpetually, just like having a child.

The mental responsibility can be constant, making it a burden.

If you are a dog guardian, you may be asking yourself... Is there enough food? Have I walked my dog enough? Am I feeding too much? Is he going to be alright if I go out for an evening? Is he going to miss me when I go away for two weeks? Is he going to be OK with his dog sitter/kennels/carer? Is he going to stop eating or mope if he does not see me? Is his barking when I am absent disturbing the neighbours? What damage will I find when I get home?

If you are a cat guardian, you may be asking yourself... I have not seen my cat for two days, has she been run over? Is she stuck in someone's garage? Is she still alive? Is she stuck in a bush somewhere? What damage am I going to find when I get home? I hear some noises downstairs, has he brought in mice again? Am I going to find half-eaten mice/birds in the kitchen? Is my beloved cat killing too much wildlife? Has my cat gotten into a fight (did he win?)? Am I feeding him too much? If I don't feed my cat more, he may leave for another home that feeds better.

If you have a bird, you may be asking yourself... Did I leave the window open? Am I feeding the right stuff? Am I providing enough mental stimulation? Is it too hot? Is it too cold?

If you have a reptile, you may be asking yourself... Have I gotten my husbandry right? Have I succeeded in creating Mother Nature in the tank in my living room? Am I doing the right thing?

These are only a few of the questions you may worry about. There are many more. The point being is that it takes up your mind space. Your energy, time and effort have been given for these mental exercises, these questions, these thoughts that are manifested in your mind because you care for your pet. Whereas they may seem innocent and harmless, if you do not balance them with rationale, common sense and perspective, they can be overwhelming. What are your thoughts (pardon the pun!) on this?

Lucy actually suffers from anxiety attacks and breakdowns (even when Lucky, her pug, is healthy) as she is concerned about her husband being stressed about the finances of a vet visit when he next becomes ill. This is when the mental responsibility of having a pet becomes a mental burden. You have to be careful that your mind remains positive when caring for your pet.

- **The things that I have to do...**

The responsibility of providing suitable food, basic shelter and engaging enrichment for your pet lies solely with you. Once you have a pet, you are completely responsible for fulfilling his physical needs.

Providing shelter or a safe haven for your pet may involve considerable expense depending on your pet and how much it is being indulged. It does not necessarily mean buying an outdoor kennel (though those costs may not be small) but even living in the house usually involves an area and a bed of some form, washing the bed and blankets or repairing the damage done to pristine furniture, brand new shoes or anything your dog may fancy chewing. Cats may ignore the rustic and practical scratching post you bought and prefer to use expensive sofas or exquisite oak table legs as scratching posts instead. You may have forgone family holidays, life-changing trips and travel opportunities in your life as you may not have been able to physically leave your pet.

The responsibility of feeding extends from merely buying basic complete nutrition to actually making sure the right food is given in the right amount at the right time. The range of pet food has increased dramatically in the past decade, making it almost a minefield for you to choose. The responsibility of the actual feeding also lies with you so planning has to be done to ensure your pet is fed at the right time. This may limit what you can do as you may need to be at home to make sure your pet is fed. You may get your neighbour or your friend to help feed your pet but it certainly is still your responsibility.

Engaging enrichment is crucial to ensure your pet's mental well-being. Having a dog involves daily walking at regular intervals and it can be challenging for you depending on your personal circumstances, working hours, health and many other factors. Keeping an African Grey parrot or a Harris Hawk would certainly involve a huge commitment to provide mental and/or physical stimulation. The African Grey parrot has been thought to have a mental capacity of a five-year-old child so interaction and enrichment is critically important to keep his mind active and reduce behavioural issues. Birds of prey like Harris Hawks will need to be flown regularly for similar reasons.

It is important that you do your research before getting your pet to ensure that you take on the (wonderful) responsibility knowingly and willingly. This will allow you to get the best out of your pet and build a fruitful, satisfying relationship. If not, it may present as an unwanted burden instead.

- **More than just a pet...**

No one can pinpoint exactly when humans first started keeping dogs as pets, but estimates range from roughly 13,000 to 30,000 years ago. What may have started as domestication and utilitarian reasons for keeping a pet have evolved into strong companionship these days.

Did you know that two thirds of Americans live with an animal, and according to a 2011 Harris poll, 90 percent of pet guardians think of their dogs and cats as members of the family? These relationships have benefits. For example, in a survey by the American Animal Hospital Association, 40 percent of married female dog guardians reported they received more emotional support from their dog than from their husband or their kids.

The research company, Kelton Global, surveyed pet guardians' attitudes toward treating dogs as family members. According to the survey's findings, dog guardians amazingly have about seven photos of their dogs on display, more than their children!

In May 2018, MoreTh>n revealed a study that found British dog guardians are spending an average of £240 on their pet each month, with costs incurred including food, treats, professional grooming, pet insurance and vets fees. Cat guardians meanwhile are spending £100 on similar items in comparison.

Explore these amazing statistics:

➢ Over a quarter of pet guardians admit they like to pamper their pets and women in particular (46%) find it hard to pass by a new toy or treat even if they did not plan on buying it. (Mintel 2015)

➢ One in five splurges £20 a month on outfits for their dog or cat. (Mintel 2015)

➢ Animal-loving Brits are spending a fortune on their furry friends with the average guardian allocating £1,150 a year – or £95 a month. (Mintel 2015)

➢ The craze for dressing up pets seems set to continue with guardians spending, on average, nearly £200 a year on clothes for their pets, with over one in five (22 per cent) admitting they spend up to £20 on outfits each month. Outfits are the third highest expenditure for dog guardians and the second highest for cat guardians, after food. (Mintel 2015)

➢ In total, the UK spends over £10 billion a year on their dogs alone and £8 billion on cats. (Mintel 2015)

➢ While eight in 10 consumers have changed their grocery shopping habits to save money, new research shows only one in 10 pet guardians have cut back on what they spend on their animals. It finds 42% would spoil pets with treats even though their budgets are tight, with more than half of dog guardians indulging their pooches with Christmas stockings. (Business independent source)

➢ 66% of guardians buy accessories for their pets including birthday and Christmas presents. 32% buy treats and gifts more often for their pets than their partners. (PetPlan Pet Census 2011)

➢ £264 is the average annual spend on presents for pets. (One Poll 2015)

➢ 27% of dog guardians get their pet spa-style treatments. (One Poll 2015)

➢ 25% of pet guardians buy their pets' birthday presents. (One Poll 2015)

➢ In the last five years spending on pet gifts has grown by £286,000,000. (One Poll 2015)

➢ Men are more likely to buy Valentine's presents for their pets. (One Poll 2015)

➢ Women are more likely to buy anniversary presents for their pets. (One Poll 2015)

➢ 88% of people admit to spending up to £50 on extravagant presents for their pets. (One Poll 2015)

We are crazy about our pets, there is no denying that. What does your pet mean to you?

• **What happens when you don't want your pet anymore?**

In 2014, there were more than 110,000 stray or abandoned dogs in the UK, with 21 dogs a day being put down by local authorities (more than 7,000 in that year). Figures from the Dogs Trust suggest more than 47,500 dogs were abandoned by their guardians in the UK in 2014. The animals all ended up in council pounds and more than 5,000 were later put down, according to the charity's annual survey of 345 local authorities.

In total, 102,363 strays were picked up by UK councils in 2014-15 – a fall from 110,675 dogs in 2013-14. Councils were putting healthy animals down due to "a lack of space and resources", the Dogs Trust said. Of the 102,363 stray dogs picked up that year, 54,767 were reunited with their guardians. However, 47,596 dogs were never picked up.

It is estimated that about 250,000 animals (of which **130,000 are dogs) come into UK rehoming charities each year.**

In 2018, there were currently 56,043 stray dogs across the UK, according to Dogs Trust's Stray Dogs Survey report. The number of strays collected by local authorities in the UK was at its lowest level in 21 years, and 15% down compared to the previous year. In the same year, RSPCA rescued and collected more than 102,900 animals.

Only 57% of the estimated stray dogs were reunited with their guardians. Microchipping pets and keeping up to date with details is vital when it comes to reuniting lost dogs, yet it has been reported that only 35 per cent of the total number of stray dogs found were microchipped. Many of the chipped dogs were still unable to be returned to their guardians due to incorrect contact details – and, in some cases, the guardians did not respond or gave the dogs up.

Have you rescued a pet before? Or have you given up your pet in the past?

• UK Pet Charities

In the UK, there are an outstanding 82 animal charities. They span from well-known ones like the Royal Society for the Prevention of Cruelty to Animals (RSPCA), Blue Cross, Dogs Trust and People's Dispensary for Sick Animals (PDSA) to smaller charities like Tiggywinkles and Buttercups Sanctuary for Goats.

There is a charity for almost every species, for example the British Hen and Welfare Trust, Cattle Health Initiative, Shark Trust, Hedgehog Care, Frogslife and Scottish Wildcat Association.

The turnover of pets in charities does depend on the charity itself. Some charities may keep animals that are unable to be rehomed and some will not. There are pros and cons to both solutions.

A charity that keeps animals that cannot be rehomed will allow those animals to continue to live. However, it does mean ongoing costs and facilities are needed to sustain long-term maintenance. For those charities that do not keep animals that are unable to be rehomed (due to health, behaviour, temperament, etc.) and are euthanised, it does allow a higher flow of animals to be brought in and rehomed, that is, they are able to help more animals.

In the latter charities, the turnover of animals is usually quite high. This means a huge amount of effort is made to ensure that the rescued animal finds a home as soon as possible so a new bond can be forged between that pet and his guardian. In addition, it also means more space is freed for another animal to be rescued at the charity in the shortest possible time. Despite the speed and efficiency, it is common practice for the charity to ensure the pet is in good health, neutered and vaccinated before rehoming.

You can help by reducing the amount of animals to be rehomed in the first place. Where some reasons are unavoidable (like death of the pet guardian), many reasons for giving up a pet are due to lack of understanding and commitment which could be avoidable.

- **Is pet 'ownership' real?**

By now, you will have found that I used the term 'guardian' instead of 'owner'. This is why...

When you own something, it belongs to you, like a toaster or a book. You expect it to do your bidding and you can do what you want with it. If you do not like it, you can give it away, store it somewhere out of sight or dispose of it.

When you have a pet, I believe you do not really own him. You are merely the guardian. You have to feed him, provide a safe shelter, give entertainment and be responsible for his well-being. You cannot give him away (you should not anyway, without serious consideration), store him away if he is annoying you and certainly disposal should never be taken lightly. *He will train you to make sure he receives what he needs.* Yes, you heard right. HE WILL TRAIN YOU.

It is almost like a child; rarely do we say we 'own' a child. We just say that he is ours. We have to take care of him and usually, we feel obliged to take care of him (we should anyway since we brought him into our lives!). The responsibility (and burden) is ours. So, it is more of a pet 'guardianship' than 'ownership'. We are pet guardians, you and I, not pet owners.

Takeaway: Pet guardianship can be complicated. It is also usually fraught with huge emotional, physical, mental and financial responsibilities and in some cases, may become a burden. You do not really 'own' your pet. You care for him and with this, comes different expectations. It usually is extremely rewarding and you will agree that having your pet has greatly improved your overall quality of life. However, pet guardianship is not for everyone and not all pets will benefit from it. An ill-conceived pet guardianship can result in them being abandoned or even destroyed, potentially physically or mentally.

WE CAN JUDGE THE HEART OF A MAN BY HIS TREATMENT OF ANIMALS.

– Emmanuel Kant

After learning about the ins and outs of pet guardians, let's now find out more about your pet's doctors... veterinarians.

I REALLY DON'T WANT TO GO

TO THE DENTIST... OR THE VETS

Working with Your Vet:

A Pleasure or Pain?

Many years ago, I went back to the town where I first started working to meet a friend (the practice manager from my previous job). We were sitting in a coffee shop just chatting and minding our own business when a man approached us and started to hurl abuse at me. "You nearly killed my cat, you evil Chinese man! You ought to be ashamed of yourself!" I was naturally taken aback. I found the man vaguely familiar. After about two to three minutes of ranting, he left. Evidently for this particular guardian, his relationship with me, his attending vet at that time, was fraught with mistrust and discontentment.

On the other hand, one of my clients drives past five

other vet practices and travels more than 30 miles to consult with me. She trusts me explicitly with her pets and working with her is an extreme pleasure. She brings gifts every time she comes in, be it some donuts or some form of nutritious delicacy. There was once when she even brought fresh croissants from France when she returned from her holidays! It may be safe to say that she enjoyed working with us.

In this chapter, we will explore the mind-set of pet guardians and vets. We will discuss how certain factors may influence whether your relationship with your vet is going to be one of pleasure or pain. We will find out why you may gel with your vet or struggle with her.

- **I use that vet practice because...**

There are many factors you would look at when choosing a vet practice. The most common reason is usually convenience. The location (how close it is to your home) and the flexibility of opening hours (evening and weekend surgery) are usually considered. Another convenience may be if the practice treated multiple species (so a farmer is likely to use the same vet that treats his cows to treat his dog).

Aside from convenience, a survey reported the three most common influences are cleanliness, friendliness and competence. It is interesting to note that new, advanced modern equipment, further certification of the vet surgeons or specialism were not the top of the list. Yet, these are what many vets are striving for at some point of their career. Vets want to pursue their interests to further their expertise. Practice owners boast of newer and more advanced equipment. Both parties may feel (not all vets are like this but most are) that is the natural advancement of career or status, making them more appealing to pet guardians, but it is clearly not true.

It may seem surprising that cleanliness is rated as the highest factor, above clinical competence. However, if you were to walk into a restaurant and find the entrance dirty with bits of food on the floor, your first impression would be to think that the place is dirty and the kitchen might also be dirty and (fairly or unfairly) conclude that the food cannot be that good.

You like to be treated nicely in general, especially in a service industry like veterinary care, so it is not surprising that friendliness is important. No one enjoys rudeness or discourteous behaviour. You are always secretly hoping to be wowed by life as there are really not many amazing services around. Especially, when you go to the vet, it is usually when your pet is unwell and a friendly face really helps to reassure even before any medical assistance is provided.

And finally, let's talk about competence. You like a professional to be able to solve your problems. That is why you seek them out and pay them for their services.

Even when some may not be able to give you instant solutions, you still expect them to be able to give you an idea what the next step is.

There are many other factors which are not as common. They include cost, specialism, personal relations, previous history, loyalty, type of service and specific reasons (like provision of PDSA services).

Certainly, you will select your vet based on what is important to you. How do you choose your vet?

- **That is not why I have a pet...**

In this chapter, the different ways guardians view their pets and in doing so, how they treat their pets, will be discussed using my experience.

How you view animals will differ greatly from others. There are countless views, attitudes and opinions when it comes to having a pet and it is not practical to cover all. These are the four common ones that I see.

1.   Kai, the Useful One:

     Have you ever had a dog that existed to perform a function or a utility like a tool or an instrument? Examples would include a sheep dog that helps the farmer to herd livestock, a police sniffer dog that is trained to detect drugs, or a trained dog that guides his blind guardian. This does not mean that you treated him solely as an instrument. You probably kept him extremely well, not unlike a family member. However, you know he exists to perform a specific role and must be good at it. If not, you may have to replace him or simply keep him as a pet rather than a working animal.

2. Casper, the Ideal One:

Perhaps, you grew up with a pet when you were a child and felt that it was a great idea as it was 'good for children' when you started your family. Mary was a guardian that had a cat because her psychiatrist advised her it was good for her mental health (she did not like cats and certainly did not bond with that particular one!). In these relationships, you may not have understood and embraced the full implications of having a pet. You may get frustrated when things are not going your way with your pet, for example, shedding hair, not being fully house trained, not achieving good recalls for your dog, holding you back from certain activities like travelling and other little things that causes 'hindrance'.

3. Flash, the Unexpected One:

Have you ever had a pet that you did not really want but obtained for various reasons that may or may not have been in your control? Eleanor is an 80-year-old lady taking care of a boisterous two-year-old, 45kg, incredibly fit German Pointer, Chaska. That monster of a beast was an extremely sweet dog but nonetheless, very strong and often took the old lady for a walk instead of the other way round! I asked her why she wanted such a strong, big dog and suggested that a smaller dog may be better suited for her. Secretly, I feared for her life! She told me that Chaska had originally belonged to her son. He had fallen off a cliff, broke his back in two places (the dog, not the son!) and had undergone intensive surgery. Her son had slept with him in the living room for two months nursing poor Chaska back to health but unfortunately, contracted some weird condition from lying on the floor for too long and died. Hence, she had 'inherited' Chaska from her late son and he holds the memory of her son for her. What a tale! I could hardly believe her story. And that is why she had that I-will-pull-you-over-one-day dog. I still fear for her today just in case he pulls her over. Last I heard, they have a great relationship and no one was injured! I have also seen where parents took over pets from their children when their children could not cope. Usually the parents are almost retired and the children are grown-ups who struggle with their pets due to their jobs, unexpected situations, accommodation or children.

Likewise, the new adopted guardians usually build strong relationships with their pets even though they did not plan to have any.

4.   Rocky, the Chosen One:

This one is special. This is the pet you have planned and researched to death for a long time and finally sought him out. You are undoubtedly dedicated and have done your due diligence. You have spoken to many professionals like vets, dog trainers and others like your breeder and other guardians who have similar pets. You probably even dreamt of your pet before even meeting him. You have a close (sometimes intense) relationship with your pet. He is treated as part of your family or sometimes even like your child. You invest a lot of time, effort, money and energy in giving him the best that is possible. You build your lives around his needs, requirements and wants. You are extremely sophisticated and will listen to no one except people that you fully trust when it comes to what is best for your pet. At your vets, you want to know all the pros and cons of each option suggested. In addition, you will endeavour to find all non-medical methods that may help your pet. In my experience, you are the sort of pet guardians I found it best to work with as you genuinely want the best (even when you disagree with me) and will do what is needed to obtain the best result for your pet, whether it is regarding their health or well-being. You will stop at nothing and do everything that is the best for him. You ROCK and don't ever change!

This list is certainly not exhaustive and it is not meant to be. Sometimes, you can see a mixture of traits in different situations and different life stages of either your pet or yourself.

Your attitude to pets can vary vastly depending on your beliefs, expectations and limitations. What sort of guardian do you think you are?

- **Dr Jekyll and Mr Hyde**

OK, maybe not that dramatic but vets can certainly display different traits. Here are some common types. Let's see if you can recognise them.

1. Sophie, the Intelligent Vet:

    She is brilliant academically and thoroughly well-informed in her field. She thrives on information, the latest research and the latest thinking. She is interested in evidence-based medicine, only choosing techniques and treatment options that have proven clinical evidence. She may not be the best at explaining things to you. In fact, she is probably in her element only when faced with challenging cases and thrives on solving the clinical problem, not necessarily your problems. She does care deeply for your pet, though she may come across as 'clinical' and 'impersonal' to you.

2. Beth, the Softie Vet:

Showing her human side is second nature when dealing with your pets and you. She is compassionate and will cry with you should the situation arise. She is good at what she does clinically. She will take time to explain things to you, making sure not to use any technical terms. You may find her a bit patronising at times but you are likely to develop a close relationship with her.

3. Susan, the Professional Vet:

She draws a very clear line between herself and you. She views your pet as an individual case and seeks not to build any further relationship with you apart from a clinically professional one. She is usually extremely competent at what she does and is a great clinician. You may sometimes misunderstand her as not being a very good vet just because her relationship appears to be purely transactional.

These are the three common traits that I see in my working life. The interesting thing (to me) is that I have found myself exhibiting the second and third traits in different stages of my career. I remember when I first graduated, I entered the 'Professional' stage. I wanted to be as professional as I could. I wanted to be taken seriously. I mistakenly thought that by showing you solely the professional side of me, I would be perceived as professional, someone who knows their craft very well and able to provide an objective judgement.

As I practised more, I began to understand how mistaken I had been. A few points emerged over time that showed me the error of my way of thinking.

1. By showing the 'non-vet' aspect of myself, I am able to be seen as more 'human' and not just a vet. In doing so, it increases rapport and trust and I get increased compliance from you resulting in better outcomes for your pet.

2. By applying the above, I actually literally become a better vet. You and your pets experience better results.

3. This way of thinking actually challenges the entire perspective of veterinary medicine which is the reason why this book was written. I truly believe that veterinary medicine is 80% human (taking care of you) and 20% animal (taking care of your pet).

4. By having the mind-set above, I find myself feeling more fulfilled and happier in my job than I have ever been. Saving and helping animals feel great but bringing positive changes to you by improving the bond between you and your pet elevates the feeling of 'great' to a whole new, different, higher level.

5. Over time, I had developed the 'Softie' vet in me. I found myself extremely interested in you, your pet's guardian. I find the bond between your pet and you exceedingly fascinating for each is beautifully unique. No two bonds are the same. I find that I am able to bring more value to you than I ever have. Sure, I find your pet's condition interesting and I enjoy diagnosing and treating diseases but learning more about you, your circumstance, what your pet means to you, how your pet's condition is affecting you and learning about you more than just as your pet's guardian, has totally changed the game for me.

There are as many vet 'characters' as there are human personalities. It is useful to understand more about your vet (depending on what are you looking for in the first place), allowing better expectations in your relationship with her. For example, if you are looking for just an expert to solve your pet's problem and do not expect any personal support, you may be happy with the

'Intelligent' or the 'Professional' type. If you are wanting a deeper relationship with a vet that understands more of you, your expectations and beliefs, perhaps a vet that exhibits a bit more of the 'Softie' side may benefit you better.

It depends on how you establish trust and competency. You may prefer to see credentials or simply be able to relate personally. What type of vet do you prefer? Or you do not really mind?

- **When I go to my vets, I am terrified of...**

After surveying 1,534 pet guardians on their fears of coming to the vets, these are the top five.

1. The fear of your pet not getting better (or dying)

2. Thinking it is your fault that your pet is ill

3. The cost of treatment

4. The time and effort needed to aid recovery of your pet (how are you going to manage?)

5. The fear of judgement from your vet

It is interesting to note that four out of five (not the first one) reasons do not involve the health of the pet. I find it interesting considering the majority of the consultation (usually) is spent on diagnosing and giving treatment and not really addressing the other four fears. In fact, 90% of my vet degree was focused on learning to diagnose and to treat. Considering your vet is treating you as much as your pet, contemplating your fears, is she even scratching the surface of her potential to help not only your pet but you, the pet guardian?

All the Vet Colleges produce vets that are usually extremely clinically competent. They are good at diagnosing and treating and most of the time, your pets do recover, hence addressing the first fear.

As for the second fear, does your vet spend enough time asking you how you feel? If you are feeling guilty of the situation, is she reassuring enough to improve your mental well-being to allow you to be a better pet guardian and also feel better about yourself? Or does she solely improve your pet's health and considers her job done?

The cost of treatment is also a valid fear to a certain extent when you are faced with unexpected costs. Has your vet found out if this is a fear of yours? Does she know what is considered too much or too little for you? Does she understand your financial situation? Or is she solely focused on her knowledge of best practice regardless the cost or worse still, projects her values and beliefs onto you? Considering this is one of the most common reasons for you to fall out with your vets, does she spend enough time educating you about her costing BEFORE you need to see her or does she try to explain a sensitive topic like money during an emotionally charged situation when your pet is sick and needs treatment?

Let's pretend cost is not a concern. You may still struggle with the treatment due to the time, effort and commitment required for your pet that may disrupt your life greatly. For example, injecting insulin twice daily for your diabetic pet may not be possible for your outdoor cat that only comes in once in a while to feed, or assisting recovery for your large Labrador after a hip replacement when you usually take your dog with you in a small van that is too small for him to turn round at sharp angles after the operation. Does your vet spend enough time understanding the situation at your home before prescribing a treatment?

The final fear is a big one. It is one that many vets may not have even considered or been aware of. What your vet says, as a professional, and how she acts with you, is paramount. If you already have the fear of being judged, you can easily be discouraged or feel you are being a bad pet guardian by how she speaks to you unintentionally. For example, if your vet had mentioned (with all the best intentions) that your pet would have benefited from being seen sooner from a purely clinical point of view, you may feel like you are being told off. Is your vet sensitive enough to understand your psyche and mental state to address those fears or is she just focused on treating your pet?

I have found that I am able to practise veterinary

medicine at a much higher level if I include you as part of my work. As in, apart from investigating, diagnosing and treating the pet, the same amount of effort and time in understanding and ultimately, treating you, the wonderful pet guardian, is important too. With that, the entire concept of veterinary medicine can be brought to a whole new degree of awareness and helping as I am not only healing your pet but healing you too.

• Fear is the Mind-Killer

Being a vet is not easy. Being any health professional is not easy. There are certainly plenty of fears and these are some common fears your vet may have (I know I did and sometimes still do).

1. The 'Am I doing the best thing for my patient?' fear. With the vast amount of knowledge and relentless advancement of veterinary medicine, it can be quite daunting for your vet to be sure that the advice and treatment given is the 'best'. With all the best intentions, your vet may fear that the advice given may not be the 'gold standard' especially if your pet does not show improvement. This can be quite unfair as there can be many methods to achieve the same result and in medicine, sometimes animals just do not recover regardless of treatment type and yet your vet may have this fear.

2. The well-known 'Imposter' Syndrome. Sometimes despite her knowledge, experience and education, she may still have the uncertainty of whether she is 'qualified' to do the job. I remember during the first six months of graduation when I was actually 'being a vet' treating animals. In the consultation room, when I was explaining the findings and treatment to the pet guardian who was nodding in agreement and understanding, a voice inside me was shouting, "Don't listen to me! I really have no idea what I am talking about!" And to my horror, they actually paid for my consultation and thanked me for it. Boy, did I feel like an imposter then. It did not matter that the advice and treatment I gave was sound and their pet got better as expected. I just felt fake. This is usually more common with fresh graduates but it can certainly still happen even to extremely experienced vets. I believe self-esteem (or the lack of) plays a major role in this fear.

3. The 'Have I let the pet guardian down?' fear. This is an interesting fear that occurs in some professions and not so much in others. Sometimes, it is more of guilt. For example, an unregistered pet guardian may have called at 2am and demanded an emergency consultation that did not take place due to various reasons (maybe they could not afford the fee, were too drunk to drive and wanted an unwarranted house visit, or any other reason). It is

not uncommon for your vet to feel guilty or just that they are letting that pet guardian and his pet down. I know there was a time when I was not able to sleep for the rest of the night after a phone call like that. Another perfect example is when the pet guardian is not able to afford treatment and either received none or the cheaper, not-as-ideal treatment. Some vets would carry that fear of letting down the pet guardian and his pet for some time. I do not recall florists or butchers feeling bad if a customer is not able to afford their premium bouquet or prime steak! (By the way, I have nothing against florists and butchers, I think they provide immense value to their customers!)

4. The 'Am I going to be struck off?' fear. All vets in UK are registered with and governed by the Royal College of Veterinary Surgeons (RCVS). There are times when a vet gets struck off from the register and is then unable to practise anymore. Usually, it is due to some form of misconduct. Naturally (or unnaturally), this fear exist with vets. "Have I done or am I about to do something that could result in me getting struck off?" or, "Is that customer going to complain about me which could result in ending my career (not merely my job)?" are questions your vet may ask herself at times.

5. The 'Are you happy with what has been done?' fear. This fear sometimes lies in the lack of or poor

communication with you, to understand your expectations and concerns when treating your pet. When that happens, even when your pet has gotten better, your vet may still think that you may not be entirely pleased with the result.

6. The 'Have I done everything and not forgotten anything?' or, 'Have I done enough?' fear. Yes, many (not all!) vets are perfectionists. They love details and the idea of a perfect treatment with a perfect outcome. As the medicine can be extremely fluid and variable, with different factors and circumstances in play, almost any treatment is custom and yet, they are still striving for perfection. So, despite doing 99% of everything that could possibly be done, sometimes, they still fear that they have missed out that 1%. Considering that nature has an amazing way of taking care of herself, this fear is usually unfounded but it may certainly affect your vet.

So, there you go. I have exposed the fears that you may not know exist but your vet may battle with constantly. It may allow you to see that she is not perfect (though she may want you to feel that!). Perhaps by sharing this knowledge with your vet, it may evoke empathy and improve mutual understanding.

- **I can't read your mind!**

Lack of or poor communication has been cited as one of the top three reasons for you to complain and also for leaving a vet practice. Considering approximately only 7% of communication is verbal (and the rest non-verbal), purely transferring verbal information is simply not adequate.

These are the top two reasons why this issue is so common.

1. You were unable to communicate your beliefs, expectations and concerns adequately due to lack of time, stress due to your pet being ill, your mistrust for your vet, being too preoccupied with other thoughts, unawareness and maybe it is just not something you do. Sometimes you may feel embarrassed to be making a fuss or presume your vet to feel the same as you. You may only reveal your concerns when specifically asked or after prolonged questioning and cajoling. A report by the Society of Practising Veterinary Surgeons (SPVS) indicated that pet guardians actually decided NOT to voice their concerns or extra conditions their pet may have if they perceived their vet to be under stress (due to lack of time or other reasons). Have you ever missed something out to help your vet when she seemed stressed?

2. Your vet fails to manage your expectations of the outcome or treatment plan advised. This is usually made harder by NOT understanding your beliefs, expectations and concerns in the first place. It is almost guesswork whether you are going to be content with the outcome. Your vet would have been very well trained regarding your pet's diagnosis and his treatment. She would find the solution to his medical problem such that when it is resolved, she might think that automatically resolves all other issues. In many cases, that could be true. However, that may not be the whole story. On top of the presenting medical condition, some issues may require your concerns and problems to be addressed and resolved as well. Some issues are not entirely medical. It is not uncommon for your vet to presume that your expectations are met once the medical issue is resolved as this is how she was trained, to solve the medical condition as a form of resolution.

This is where vets may fall short because in Vet College, they are not adequately trained in interpersonal skills and customer communication. They focus mainly on animals only. In doing so, the above reasons are made more obvious.

Like many relationships, poor or lack of communication does not usually result in favourable outcomes. Your vet and you need to be brave and take responsibility for clear, specific communication with the intention to actually understand each other to enable an effective relationship that has beautiful results.

- **There is not enough time!**

Many first opinion vet practices provide 10-15 minutes for a consultation. This time is used to take a clinical history, perform a clinical examination, administer and discuss the treatment and write notes.

Breaking it down, it would take about 2-3 minutes to ask questions about your reason(s) for bringing your pet in, another 4-5 minutes to perform the clinical examination on your pet, maybe another 4-5 minutes prescribing and putting up the medication/giving injections/explaining about the condition and leaving perhaps 2-3 minutes to write the notes up in your pet's record. No time has been allocated for any contingency, understanding your wishes and intentions, much less bonding. It is almost like getting married on the first date!

Some issues like a broken claw may take less time but many would take longer.

For example, let's pretend that your pet needed an operation to remove a mass. To explain the reason for surgery, managing your expectations, discussing finances and actually give you time to absorb and understand all of above in a few minutes can be quite daunting.

(Especially if your vet does not understand your beliefs, expectations and concerns.) Your vet may get stressed as she knows she has limited time to explain everything (even with the best intention of wanting to tell you more but she can't or maybe she can but would have to rush it). You may get stressed needing to make decisions on the spot as you have not had a chance to understand, much less absorb and digest the facts or more specifically, do not know or like, much less trust your vet that provided the advice. It is tough.

It is not easy to gain mutual understanding, much less form a bond in such a limited time. It is a big ask for both your vet and you to be discussing major (or even minor) treatments and procedures if there was not a common shared impression to begin with. A true working relationship with reciprocal recognition is challenging in the short time allocated for interaction.

It is no wonder your perception of what value your vet brings may differ greatly to what she may actually wish to provide.

- **The Perfect Set-Up for Disaster**

How many people would select to live with their spouse on the first date? How many people would buy a house on the first viewing? How many people would buy the first car presented (without a test drive)? Would you?

It is not unusual for you (especially if your pet is very

young) to be disinterested in spending time with your vet due to the nature of what veterinary medicine means (ill health and unwell pets). It would be uncommon for you to be well versed in medical conditions, the implications, the diagnostic approach and management or treatment of medical conditions. If you are enthusiastic, you may bring your pet in for his yearly vaccination and possibly a six-month check in between. These consultations can be briefly clinical and sometimes the six-month check may not even be with your vet.

The next time that you bring your pet to your vet could be when your pet is critically ill. If you are lucky, you may see a familiar face. If not, it could be another vet who is a stranger. That is hardly the time to be building trust or bonding and yet, you are expected to make difficult decisions on the spot that may involve multiple factors and potentially great cost. Making such decisions is never easy, especially when unprepared.

It is almost an unfair responsibility placed on both your vet and you in those circumstances. Your vet has to explain a potentially complicated condition, asking you to invest in further tests, offer a choice of treatment compounded with pros and cons, make you aware of the (possibly high) costs involved and expect you to make the right choice. You then have to make hard choices on matters that may be foreign to you, sometimes at short notice for emergencies, accept whatever costs that are involved (due to ignorance of how much medical costs are and the emotional desire to see your pet's health improve). Also, you have to feel confident you can trust the professional standing in front of you (most people have no issue trusting a professional but you may naturally have doubts when there is no prior relationship to build upon) and to feel confident that you are making the right choice. You also have to accept the vast responsibility that you are the one who will decide your pet's outcome with the choices you make now.

Now, if that is not a recipe for a disaster to happen, what is?!

Imagine your vet is your close friend, someone who knows and understands you, someone with whom you have had conversations about your beliefs and expectations regarding your pet's health and someone who is aware of the bond you have with your pet. She knows your financial situation and understands any limitation (may not relate to money) you have in helping your pet recover. In addition, you know her beliefs and expectations match yours. You understand what she stands for and the approach she takes in helping your pet and you. You know her intentions well. If a relationship like this existed, would the outcome of the above situation be better? Would it be easier to make important decisions, even if you do not understand the details, with confidence that not only your beliefs and expectations are taken into account but also the unique bond you have with your pet is considered? This is more likely to lead to better results for all four parties, your pet, you, your vet and by extension, the vet profession itself.

This does involve time and effort being invested from the start. It is best when there is nothing wrong with your pet so there is no pressure on any decisions to be made. It is purely by choice to ensure a common understanding is shared between your vet and you so when the time comes to make difficult choices, they can be made with better clarity, increased confidence and less fear.

The challenge lies in shifting mind-sets. At present, it is uncommon for you or your vet to invest the time, effort and energy when your pet is healthy. Only by investing in building a bond, can a true working relationship be formed resulting in better outcomes (just like any relationship!). That simply cannot be achieved by only seeing your vet when something has gone wrong and medical treatment is needed for your pet.

• I was so stressed, I can't remember anything!

When you bring your ill pet in, you may be so stressed that you are simply not able to process any form of information given, understand any options presented and much less to make an informed decision. It is not uncommon for you to state that you actually did not understand the content of the consent form you had signed despite your vet or nurse repeating and emphasising, as you were simply too stressed at that moment to take anything in. This is very typical.

I have been accused of faking a pet guardian's signature on the consent form! The stress that he underwent literally made him forget he had ever signed or consented to anything.

The above is less likely to happen if there was a good relationship built on trust and integrity between your vet and you.

- **Not good enough, I expected more!**

As veterinary medicine improves over the decades, with the rise of specialism and modern equipment, it means advanced procedures that were unheard of have become possible. Examples of these advancements would include the relatively more common use of Magnetic Resonance Imaging (MRI) and Computed Tomography (CT), advanced spinal surgery, Total Hip Replacements (THR), keyhole surgery, improved drugs for chemotherapy and treatment, stem cell therapy and improved diagnostic capabilities.

Social media and television documentaries on these improvements may have raised your awareness so it is unsurprising that your expectations may have dramatically increased.

You may be more demanding compared to fifty years ago and rightly so you should. That is called modernisation.

However, for other pet guardians who do not demand these technical advancements and expertise, there are other requirements that their vets may not provide.

As discussed, your vet is extremely well trained in the anatomy, physiology, diagnostic approach and treatment of your pet but not as well in the other aspects (mainly relating to you). What she may sometimes fail to provide is emotional, psychological and pastoral support.

For example, you may wish to check if your pet is still protected against the diseases vaccination protects before revaccinating or simply discuss the need to vaccinate in the first place but your vet may not be open to those ideas. Similar views can be said for flea, tick and/or worm treatments.

Or you may wish to keep your dog intact/entire (not neutered) but it may not be what your vet would advise.

Sometimes, you desire alternative treatments like homeopathy, Bowen technique, acupuncture, but she may not provide or support those treatments.

There are times when your real issue extends beyond the superficial ailment your pet is having but your vet may not pick that up for it is not what she was trained to do. She is not able to see past the problem in your pet and sometimes, that is the problem. She has helped your pet but not you.

She may be thinking, *That is not my problem. I am only interested in treating the dog (or cat),* or, *We are vets, we are not in charge of sorting you out, only your pet!* It is common to think that, I used to be one of them.

Now, I believe that your vet has been given the gift of treating animals. She is in a position of power to bring much more value and goodness than just treating your pet(s). She has brought plenty of goodwill by treating your pet(s) already. Imagine the increased amount of goodness she can provide just by focusing a similar amount of energy on you. We can all learn. I have found it massively rewarding personally.

Sometimes the issue does not only lie with your pet. As your vet, she should be extending her diagnostic capabilities and treatment options to include the pet guardian, you. Medicine is not just medical.

- **My cousin is my vet!**

Family and friends find it difficult to accept me as an established, experienced vet that is capable of providing value to my customers and patients. I know it sounds silly but it seems that because they have watched me grow and saw me when I was not as established as present, it is difficult for them to let go of their past memory of me and accept the current version. It is almost like how a child will always remain a child in her parents' eyes, no matter how old she is.

When working with friends and family, they may be the worst customers to follow instructions, take advice and sometimes even to pay. It is not uncommon that they will be the ones who will ask for 'mates' rate' too and impose unreasonable demands.

So, would you find a friend or family to be your vet (if you know one)? If you did, would you find it difficult to listen to them, take their advice, understand their value and pay them in full? Knowing what you know about their past, would you be able to take them seriously without qualms, the way you would with other professionals?

If your answers are resounding 'yeses!', then you may work with your vet who is also your friend and/or relative without issues, just like other professional relationships *with added value.*

If you answer is 'not sure' or 'no', it may not be a good idea.

Being friends with your customers is important. There seems to be a huge difference when you make friends after they had experienced you in a professional context, compared to them knowing you before who you are now. It is just an interesting observation.

A suggestion would be to have a frank discussion with your vet friend or family about your expectations, beliefs and values to ensure a good match. Perhaps including the expectation of fees would be helpful as well. If not, there could be risk that a sour relationship could develop.

- **I am not going to tell you my thoughts... until it is too late**

It is uncommon that you (and your vet) state very clearly what your expectations are when you meet for the first time. It does depend on your personality and perhaps, your culture.

A perfect example would be dating. On the first date, you would prefer to be nice and pleasant. You would try not to be too controversial and upset your date. Over time, you express more beliefs, values and expectations. Like maybe whether you are vegetarian, views on children or pets, where you want to live, likes and dislikes. Your date might do the same. When that happens, you can consider whether it is a good fit (so continuing) or not (leading to a break-up). You may argue that it is easier to ask all those questions, express all beliefs and find out on the first date so less time is wasted and I will be the first to agree with you. It all makes sense and it is simple to see the logic.

However, when it comes to your relationship with your vet, very often there is no common understanding of each other's expectations and nothing is said until your pet is ill. When medical treatment is needed, those situations may be emotionally charged and it is harder to establish mutual understanding then. Or when beliefs clash (like views on vaccinations, neutering, feeding), conversations and discussions may not take place and trust may erode rapidly.

These situations occur often. It is usually the lack of vital communication and building of trust that ends up in mistrust and dispute. Unlike the couple that are dating and have the opportunity to voice their expectations over time, it is not often you (and your vet) would spend the time to question if the relationship is a good fit or not, or whether it is likely to result in a negative outcome.

Without communication, you are forced to work with much more (likely to be inaccurate) assumptions. Mutual understanding between you and your vet should be improved to enable a more fulfilling and complete relationship. Both parties need to take courage and initiative in establishing a fundamental foundation to build the rapport on. With that solid structure in place, your vet can provide much more than just pure medical care for your pet(s). She can also give emotional and mental support to you.

Takeaway: How coherent the relationship you have with your vet is, can vary due to many factors. It often involves mutual understanding and respect which can take time to foster. It also depends on exactly what the expectations are of each party from the other. You and your vet tend to work well together if you share the same beliefs in pet care. It takes time to like and trust each other. It can be even more challenging if no effort or time is spent fostering the understanding, earning the respect and building the trust. If you wish to foster a deeper relationship with your vet, have conversations to share beliefs and expectations of her. It may sound weird but if you are brave and voice your desire to do so, your vet may thank you for it!

THE SINGLE BIGGEST PROBLEM ABOUT COMMUNICATION IS THE ILLUSION THAT IT HAS TAKEN PLACE.

– George Bernard Shaw

A large factor that affects your relationship with your vet would be her knowing about your beliefs and expectations. Your vet may think she is in charge of your pet's health. Should the responsibility of your pet's health be your vet's or yours? Read on and explore the answer in the next chapter...

DON'T TELL ME WHAT

TO DO WITH MY PET!

The Pet Guardian as CEO:

You Are in Charge!

"Stop telling me what to do with my dog!" Mrs Jones exclaimed after being prompted by her vet (and nurses and receptionists) for the tenth time to neuter her dog. Max is a well-balanced 18-month-old Hungarian Vizsla. Many have commented on his calm and solid personality as much as how rich and deep his beautiful red coat is. Mrs Jones is well aware of the pros and cons of castration. She has made an informed decision to keep Max entire (not castrated).

Here, we will challenge the mindset of your vet and you (your wonderful pet's guardian) to find out who should be in charge of your pet.

• Are you the boss?

Do you feel you are completely charge when you bring your pet to your vet? Do you feel relaxed and calm, knowing that YOU are in TOTAL CONTROL of the outcome and situation of what happens to your pet? Are you able to dictate exactly what you expect and want to see happen? Do you take responsibility of the results, whatever they may be? Do you feel you make all decisions mindfully and nothing will be done without your express and informed choice? If you say, 'Hell yeah!' to all questions above, congratulations! You are the rare far and few between! If not, why not? It is after all, your pet!

Currently, you may bring your pet to your vet because he is not well and seek advice. The problem may be instantaneously solved or may require further investigation or treatment. Your pet may get better or (God forbid) not. When he gets better, you relax and may invest in a bit more time to find out what happened and if it can be prevented in future. If he does not get better, you may continue listening to your vet and hope that things work out. Or you may seek a second opinion and hope your problem is solved then. Fingers crossed.

How do you feel? Do you feel you are in control? Or are you at the mercy of your vet?

- **I am the Captain of his Fate and Master of his Destiny**

Princess Robin Starbuck Soloway Farmanfarmaian wrote an amazing book, *The Patient as CEO*. It talks about how patients should be in charge of their own health care and not leave the fate up to their doctors and other professionals.

Your pet belongs to you. Just like how a Chief Executive Officer (CEO) of a company that has many departments like marketing, sales, finance, human resource and administration who do their respective jobs and report back to her so the company is run as a single entity, you should do the same with your pet. You are your pet's CEO. You should be in charge of whatever happens to him, in all aspects. Why would you give up responsibility for something that important? Your vet, trainer, behaviourist and dog walker should all be working for you, not the other way round.

You would not give up control of who you see, what you wear, when you play or how you speak. Why should you give up control for your pet?

Any advice given to you or your pet should fundamentally serve you. You should be doing what is right for your pet, not because someone tells you to do so. Just like how you take care of your body, you can take care of your pet with the same diligence.

Your pet and you are unique. Remember that you spend

more time with your pet than anyone else. No professional (including your vet) or expert is ever going to be more knowledgeable about him or you than you. Ever. Bar none. Yes, work with them but always remember you are the expert of your life and your pet's life. Make their advice work for you.

Professionals only know what they are taught. Vets learn about medicine, behaviourists learn about behaviour, trainers learn about training, breeders know about breeding and pet shop keepers know about pet food. Nobody knows you and your pet better than you. Always remember that. Take charge.

Here are some tools that are available for you to be in charge.

- **Google**

In the past, there were textbooks that you could buy. You could read and sift through the jargon and understand more (if you could be bothered or had the time to do so!). Knowledge was exclusive to those who received the education (usually paid) either in university or apprenticeship. It was usually passed through the spoken word, i.e. someone had to tell you about it if you were not privy to the information before. That time has come and passed. Google launched in 1998 and since then, the way information is shared has changed.

Google is a wonderful tool and at the same time, a

complete waste of time and possibly destructive if used wrongly. Knowledge has never been more abundant and available at your fingertips. Instantly, you can find out the different causes of excessive drinking (Polydipsia) and excessive urination (Polyuria) to characteristics of a squamous cell carcinoma (a type of cancer). Or maybe you are interested in the components of a vaccination, the side effects of any drug, and clinical signs of acromegaly (excessive growth hormone). Your eight-year-old niece can find that out for you!

Google has almost made any knowledge-based value redundant and obsolete. It is not unfair to say that if you conducted research into any topic regarding the health of your pet with finesse and understanding, you would certainly be more knowledgeable in that particular topic than your vet. Your vet is only human. With the vast amount of knowledge in the world, it is impossible (and inhuman!) to know everything at any one time. New research is presented often and previous results are debunked or contradicted frequently. Even your vet uses Google! Dr Google has made the exclusivity of knowledge disappear. The playing field is almost completely levelled. You no longer need to go to your vet for information. (I no longer had to go to the library to review research papers. No more trudging through thick dusty pages!) Knowledge is no longer exclusive. Anyone with access to the internet is included in the club.

Now the downside. It's been said that 'Knowledge is abundant but wisdom is scarce.' With Google, the cost of entry to acquiring knowledge is extremely low, so everyone can access the knowledge and be 'knowledgeable'. Just like martial arts or playing a musical instrument, just because you know all the moves or all the keys on a piano, it does not mean that you can defend yourself or play Mozart. It is important to be able to sieve and filter through the information available as you will be presented with information written by anyone. In the past, there usually was a village idiot. He was recognised for what he was (an idiot) and not much attention was paid to him. Now, internet has made the village idiot global. Loads of inaccurate information is present too. It has never been more cluttered, disorganised and contradictory. For any evidence supporting a fact, there may be the same amount of contradictory evidence. The more you dig, the more you find (or get lost). Knowledge no longer equates to clarity.

Finesse and prudence are required to enable useful information to be obtained. Guidance is needed to know not 'what' but 'how' to gather information. Avoid Facebook pages or social media in general (unless it belongs to an official body like your vets or a professional organisation and even then, take information with a pinch of salt!). You can look at information provided by reputable organisations like the British Small Animal Veterinary Association (BSAVA), the British Veterinary Association (BVA) and such. Your vet may direct you to more useful and reliable sites.

Basically, there is lots of free information available to you, to enable you to understand your pet and his condition(s). Those days where information is only privy to a few are over. Learn and practice empowering yourself to be in charge of your pet. However, beware of the false information present! Remember that the information gathered must serve your pet and you. If not, it could be a waste of time at best or even harmful in some situations.

- **YouTube**

YouTube is the second most used search engine after Google. The information is presented in video format. You can learn about raw feeding, how to groom your dog, best dog beds to buy and all sorts from there. Similarly to Google, anyone can post information so beware of who you are watching. Learning from a vet or vet-based channel may be helpful. Do beware that the information given is usually that person's opinion (vet or non-vet) and there may have been advances since that content was published.

Prudence and diligence are required to ensure useful information gathered serves your pet and you.

• Examining your pet yourself

I am going to tell you a secret. Before Vet College, most vet students (myself included) had no idea how to perform a clinical examination. We did not know how to count heart rate, much less listen to the quality of heart sounds or perform a lameness workup to find out which leg is lame doing certain activities. We did not know how to check hydration status or take a temperature. All of these skills are taught and hence, can be learned. Nobody is born with skills. We learn them. That is the good news.

Please note that I am not trying to make a vet out of you. It takes years of training and experience to be good at a job and you will not replace your vet. However, you are able to do a lot of basic examinations on your pet. You do not need to know how to examine every pet like vets do but you can certainly understand more about your pet!

I am going to share with you some techniques and tips to examine your dog or cat so you can be in a better position than before to assess his health. There are further content for exotic species below.

First of all, it is extremely important for you to be practicing these techniques to gather information when your pet is well and healthy. So, when he falls ill, you can see the difference. It is hard to know what bad looks like when you do not know what good looks like.

You have nothing to compare with. Besides, different pets have different 'normal' values. Just like how your heart rate may be different from your friend's even though you are both doing the same thing. You need to find out what your pet's 'normal' is. It also gives you the opportunity to practice how to do it. Just like cycling, it will only get easier each time you do so.

Looking at his behaviour –

You know how your pet behaves better than anyone else in the world as no one else spends more time with him than you. If you think he is being less active, showing signs of unusual behaviour or feel something is just not right, you are probably correct to think that something is wrong. Believe in yourself and be brave to say that to your vet. Most vets would rather err on the side of caution than presume all is well.

(*Flex was a super bouncy Flat-Coated Retriever that greeted me with great enthusiasm. His guardian had commented that he was just not jumping high enough and hence felt something was wrong. It turned out that he had a twisted necrotic small intestine and needed immediate surgery. I would never have felt that Flex was unwell considering how bright he acted but his guardian knew better.*)

Checking the breathing –

You can count the number of breaths per minute by purely observing, without touching your pet. Look at the ribs and count how many times they rise (and fall) in a minute. Make sure you are counting each rise and fall as ONE breath. You can also observe how much effort is needed for each breath. Just like when we are healthy, breathing should be fairly effortless.

Tip – You can count the number of breaths your pet takes in 15 seconds and multiply that number by four to obtain breaths per minute instead of waiting for a full minute.

IT IS IMPORTANT TO KNOW WHAT NORMAL IS FOR YOUR PET SO PLEASE PRACTISE THIS TECHNIQUE WHEN YOUR PET IS WELL.

Checking the heart –

Depending on size of your pet, you may be able to listen to his heart by placing your ear on his chest. Usually, a stethoscope would be necessary (you can obtain them online and the prices vary from less than £5 to hundreds depending on quality. You just need a simple one!). By placing the stethoscope just behind the elbow on the chest in a dog or cat, you can usually hear the heart. You can then count the heart rate by counting the number of times the heart beats in a minute.

Tip – You can count the number of heart beats in 15 seconds and multiply that number by four to obtain the heart rate instead of waiting for a full minute.

IT IS IMPORTANT TO KNOW WHAT NORMAL IS FOR YOUR PET SO PLEASE PRACTISE THIS TECHNIQUE WHEN YOUR PET IS WELL.

Checking how well blood is flowing in your pet –

Also known as 'perfusion', this check tells you how well blood is flowing in your pet or more importantly, whether oxygen is being transported to the organs of your pet as expected. Raise his lip and look for pink areas (no colouring or pigment) on the inner lip or the gums. Observe the colour of pink. It should be a light to moderate pink. If it is deep red or pale white, it could be an issue. I would advise that to be checked out by your vet. Apply light pressure on the lip or gums and release. Once released, count the time it takes for the area to return to its original pink colour. It should be less than two seconds.

IT IS IMPORTANT TO KNOW WHAT NORMAL IS FOR YOUR PET SO PLEASE PRACTISE THIS TECHNIQUE WHEN YOUR PET IS WELL.

Checking the hydration –

These are two techniques to check if your pet is dehydrated or not. Firstly, raise his lip and touch his gums. It should be moist (normal) and not bone dry (possibly dehydrated). Secondly, you can gently pinch his skin behind his head (where your vet usually gives injections), lift up and release. Observe how fast his skin falls back into the original place. If it is slower than usual, it may indicate dehydration.

IT IS IMPORTANT TO KNOW WHAT NORMAL IS FOR YOUR PET SO PLEASE PRACTISE THIS TECHNIQUE WHEN YOUR PET IS WELL.

Checking the temperature –

The most reliable method to know your pet's temperature is from its bottom (rectally). You can buy a simple human thermometer from a pharmacy or online. It usually costs less than £10. You may apply a bit of lubricant (you can use KY jelly or any medical lubricant) so it goes into the bottom smoothly. Your pet's temperature may be obtained that way. I have found that temperature obtained from a microchip or from the ear tends not to reflect the actual temperature (it could be 1-4 degrees Celsius lower than core temperature). It is preferable to take the temperature when your pet is resting as exercise may falsely increase the temperature. The normal range for a dog or cat is about 38C to 39C.

IT IS IMPORTANT TO KNOW WHAT NORMAL IS FOR YOUR PET SO PLEASE PRACTISE THIS TECHNIQUE WHEN YOUR PET IS WELL.

Checking the weight –

It is a great idea to check your pet's weight regularly. If you are planning to diet your pet, whether to increase or decrease weight, I would advise weighing him every two weeks. If your pet is of perfect body condition, I would advise weighing once a month. If you have a small dog (that you can carry) or a cat, I would suggest using your bathroom scales. Carry your pet and obtain the total weight, subtract your own weight (by putting your pet down!) and record the difference. If you have a larger dog, I would recommend weighing him at your vets. It would also allow him to go to your vets without being poked around, which may allow him to feel more comfortable there!

Checking the Body Condition Score (Dogs and Cats) –

This is more important than the weight as the correct weight really depends on the shape and size of your pet, just like your ideal weight may not be someone else's despite being of similar age, height or size. Please refer to charts online for guidance. Simply Google 'body condition score for dogs (or cats)'.

Rabbits, guinea pigs and chinchillas –

These pets are slightly more challenging. Being prey animals, they need to show strength (vital health) and not weakness (ill health). They are great at hiding their illness and thus, you may not know that they need medical help until it is too late.

Some techniques above can be used (like checking the breathing, heart rate, temperature). It may be a bit trickier to look at exercise levels (though you may do an excellent job by being ultra-observant). A simple way of monitoring their health would be to observe their poop (the faecal output). When they are healthy, you should pay attention to three aspects of their poop – how much they poop, the size of the poop and how hard/dry (or soft/wet) their poop is. When you are familiar with the normal, any difference in those three aspects may indicate illness. You may notice them before any other visible signs.

Reptiles, birds, amphibians, invertebrates –

Depending on species, monitoring their health may be challenging using the above techniques! However, there are a couple of great practices that would be invaluable for you and your vet. Keeping a diary is useful to track conditions and provide a clear objective history, providing invaluable information about your pet. It should include his weight, what, when and how much food was fed, how often he poops (defecates)/urinates and note down any abnormalities. Any changes should be recorded, like when the enclosure was cleaned (and what with), when he last shed, lightbulb changes, any external incident that may be relevant (e.g. house move, etc.).

Diabetes

Having a pet with diabetes can be challenging and daunting. Not only are you unaware of your pet's current blood glucose level, he is relying on you to inject a fixed amount of insulin twice daily. If he misses a meal, only eats half of it or is unwell, you are unsure if you should inject the insulin or call your vet. You are unclear whether it is due to diabetes or other reasons. It can be stressful. Not after you have learnt this!

Did you know that you can check his blood glucose level in the comfort of your own home?

You can obtain a glucometer (a small handheld machine

that tells you the blood glucose level) from your vet or even Amazon. Please bear in mind that different glucometers may give slightly different readings. It is extremely important to use the same meter for the same pet. The trend is more important than the absolute value.

PLEASE DO CONSULT WITH YOUR VET FOR EXACT DETAILS ON HOW TO INTERPRET READINGS BEFORE YOU START.

The point being is that you can do it and arguably, you SHOULD do it. If your dog (or cat) should have a 'funny' episode or does something abnormal (like collapsing), with your glucometer, you can find out what his blood glucose level is and determine if the issue is due diabetes or something else. More importantly, when you call your vet, you would be able to give her this useful information which will result in more relevant and effective advice to be received.

Flea check

You can check your cat, dog or rabbit for fleas with a simple two-step process. Step one, using a flea comb (you can buy it in any large pet shop or online). Usually, the easiest and most effective location to comb is the top of the back near the tail base. That is the classic place where fleas hide out. Step two, tap the contents of the flea comb on a damp/wet piece of white paper. If there are live fleas seen or black dirt turning red, it is probably flea dirt (poop) and it would indicate your pet has a flea infestation. Please speak to your vet for treatments and recommendations. Resolving a flea infestation may not be as straight forward as you think!

Worm count

You can send off your dog or cat's faeces to get it professionally checked for certain worms (wormcount.com). (*Please note that lungworm may be missed using above method. You need a blood test for that. Most guardians would treat for lungworm if concerned as it may not be easy to detect it.*) If there are any, please speak to your vet for treatments and recommendations.

• Be more demanding!

Remember that it is your pet. You are the CEO of your pet. Make sure you are getting everything you want for your pet. At least make appropriate, informed decisions by demanding more knowledge and information. You are able to do so by approaching your vet, other paraprofessionals or learning it yourself. Professionals and paraprofessionals exist to help you and your pet, not the other way round.

Cynthia went to the salon to have her hair coloured. At the start, she chose a colour. However, when the dye was applied to her hair, the outcome was not what she had in mind. She was too embarrassed to speak out and she sat there watching her hair slowly changing to a colour she did not like or want. The hair dresser carried on for the next hour as he did not know otherwise and felt he was doing a great job with his customer's permission. In the end, Cynthia regretted it deeply as she felt she could and should have said something. She had an hour to pick any moment but she did not. Remember, you should ALWAYS feel (and be) in charge and in control. It is your pet. Both he and you depend on it.

Key takeaway: Just like your body that you take complete charge of, your pet belongs to you too. Do not compromise, be more demanding and stay in control. You would not let someone else make decisions about things that matter to you. Why would you make exceptions for your pet?

TO BE IN CHARGE IS CERTAINLY NOT ONLY TO CARRY OUT THE PROPER MEASURES YOURSELF BUT TO SEE THAT EVERYONE DOES SO TOO.
– Florence Nightingale

So, if you are in charge of your pet, what happens when your vet disagrees with you? Let's find out...

IT'S MY PET, PLEASE RESPECT

MY IDEAS AND DECISIONS

Your Rights and Entitlements

A pet guardian from Thailand who owned a 12-year-old, cancer-ridden, emaciated Labrador who could barely stand once said to me, "Being a Buddhist, I do not believe in euthanasia for it is a sin to take a life." I attempted to discuss the quality of life of his dog and how it would be easing his suffering but it was in vain.

When you have a pet, you do own your pet and they will be subjected to your beliefs and opinions, well intended or not. You have your own set of ideas and expectations. In this chapter, we will find out the common beliefs of pet guardians and vets. We will also explore what happens and how often the beliefs are not in alignment with either party.

- **I Disagree!**

Vaccination

There are usually three areas that cause contention — whether to vaccinate, when to vaccinate and what to vaccinate against. Vaccination can be considered to be introducing a foreign agent into an otherwise healthy, well-loved pet so it is natural that you may be apprehensive about it. Vaccinations have also shown to (albeit rarely) cause adverse reactions in a small number of animals. Many diseases protected by vaccination are much rarer now due to successful vaccination campaigns in the past. This success could be hindering your compliance now as you may question the need if you have not seen those particular diseases before.

Tip: Having a frank discussion with your vet about what diseases are being vaccinated against, the risk factors, the side effects and how often it needs to be done will allow an informed decision to be made by you.

I have a client called Mary who has extremely strong views against vaccination as her last dog died after a routine vaccination injection. She has dedicated many hours researching about dog vaccination. Apart from her views on that, she is extremely pleasant and receptive to all other veterinary treatments. Her vet and her work closely with immense mutual respect to provide the best for her dogs.

Neutering

Choosing a surgical procedure by choice when your pet is healthy can be quite daunting and stressful. Subjecting your healthy beloved pet to a general anaesthetic and surgical procedure can be considered a major decision especially if you do not have access to all knowledge available to make an informed decision. It is not uncommon for your information to differ from your vet's advice. Another common topic for contention is when to do it, that is, how old your pet should be before he is neutered. There can be varying opinions from other pet guardians, veterinary surgeons and para-professionals like dog trainers.

Tip: Having a frank discussion with your vet about your concerns, the pros and cons of neutering your pet, will allow you to make an informed decision.

Feeding

In the past, before the commercialisation of pet food, pet guardians tended to feed their dogs and cats leftovers. When manufactured dog and cat food was made available, it provided peace of mind for many pet guardians as they now had something specific to provide their pets without worrying about whether they were giving the right food. It also made feeding pets more convenient as the food came in bags or tins. This industry grew exponentially due to the increased demand and with time; the choices also exploded. Currently, there are dry kibble, wet tinned food, grain-free diets, prescription diets, raw feeding and even vegetarian options for dogs. This growth also made many think more about choosing the right food. In the past, feeding was just about keeping your pet alive and going whereas now, it is about wanting to provide the best food (according to your beliefs and expectations). Here is where your idea of 'best' food for your pet may not be your vet's.

Tip: Having a frank discussion with your vet about the pros and cons of different types of pet food will allow an informed decision to be made by you. Telling her why you have done so may allow her to support you better.

Entitlement

Do you consider your pet an entitlement or a luxury? This is an extremely controversial topic that has divided many. You may consider it to be a luxury, an extra expense that needs to be planned for, budgeted for in terms of time, energy, money and the ability to provide all your pet's needs. It is like owning an extra house or a yacht; it is great to have but not essential. Or eating ice-cream would be considered a luxury (though you may think otherwise!). On the other hand, you may feel that you deserve a pet whether it is affordable or not, or simply ignoring what the potential costs could be (not just involving money but time and effort as well). You would probably agree that having a pet would bring joy and happiness, improving your life, hence you feel that it is an entitlement.

You may think that as long as you provide the best that you can for your pet, it is acceptable. The difficulty lies in the definition of 'best for them'.

Tip: Make sure you have a realistic budget for your pet's health. You can discuss with your vets which pets are more prone to what diseases before getting one.

Cost of medicine

You may consider vet bills to be expensive. There are several reasons why this could be. In UK, the existence of the NHS has made the entire nation not have a poor concept but actually NO concept of medical value. So, if you are not aware of the cost of medical facilities, any fee can be considered high as there is no perception of 'normal'. This is an area where your vet may be able to share with you the cost of veterinary medicine in terms of money and intangible values.

Many vet practices operate on the 'magic door' method. You may have seen the 'magic door' yourself. Imagine bringing your pet to the consultation room where you had a chat with your vet. Shortly after, your pet walks through the 'magic door' for the planned procedures to be done (like a spay, blood test, surgical procedure, etc.) and is returned to you (walking through the 'magic door' into the consultation room) later. So it would appear to you that the door is 'magical' as your pet went through with issues and came out with the issues resolved. I have found that time spent documenting the procedures and explaining to you, the pet guardian, after the surgery does wonders in terms of building trust, bonding and providing value.

Tip: This topic is covered greater in detail later in Money, Money, Money – It's a Rich Vet's world... or is it?

Euthanasia

Do you remember the last time your pet had to be put to sleep? Did you think you assessed his quality of life well and made the right, timely decision?

There may be times when your vet may feel your pet's quality of life is compromised but you do not. There could a specific reason why you are not ready to let go. Trevor is an 18-year-old cat with kidney failure who was not eating and losing weight despite the supportive treatment provided (mentioned in first chapter). His guardian told me that his mother has senile dementia and Trevor is the only thing keeping her alive as he is the only thing she recognises and chats to on a daily basis.

Another situation occurred when I was in Thailand volunteering my vet services where a puppy was hit by a car and there was irreparable brain damage (the skull was cracked open). Euthanasia is against their religion (Buddhism) and it is preferable to let the animal die of natural causes even if it means there is suffering (sometimes a vast amount) involved. In those situations, they triggered strong feelings of conflict and psychological distress for me. I was forced to behave in ways contrary to my personal beliefs.

On the other hand, there are situations when a healthy animal is brought in to be euthanised. It is usually due to change of circumstances but it certainly does not make it easier. Once, I was sent to a farm house and had to euthanise four farm cats as the owners were moving away and not able to take them. Their ages ranged from 12 to 16 years old and they had been on the farm their whole lives and lived completely outdoors. It was felt that they could not be rehomed as it would cause too much stress and it was kinder to put them to sleep. That was not an easy task.

Tip: A further chapter on euthanasia has been dedicated to this less discussed topic.

• Seeing eye to eye

There is no study that shows how often vets disagree with pet guardians. However, in my experience, disagreements certainly do occur and can be distilled down to these few factors or a combination of them. When you disagree with your vet, it is usually due to differences in personal beliefs and expectations, your past experiences and unexpected costs (more specifically, your perception of value).

Personal beliefs and expectations –

You are shaped by what surrounds you. What makes you different from others makes you unique. It could be cultural, religious, how you were brought up and influences you received from the people you interact with. Sometimes, the difference could be so great that it could seem as though you (and your vet) are speaking a different language and a gross mistake would be to take it personally. It is very easy to feel threatened and misunderstood when your vet does not seem to accept your way of thinking. Perhaps, it may be helpful to remind yourself that your vet could be feeling exactly the same way.

I remember having a very long conversation with Max, a

Thai vet, on the topic of euthanasia. As a Buddhist, he finds the act of euthanasia immoral, distasteful and impossible to perform. He did not harbour any ill intentions and in fact, his intentions were perfect. Imagine the conversation I had with him when a puppy laid badly injured after being run over by a car, had sustained two broken legs, a severe head injury, and was unconscious. This was in Thailand and the puppy was a stray. His plan (with the best intentions and strong belief that it was the right thing to do) was to allow the puppy to naturally pass away. My gut instinct (with the best intentions and all that my training supported) was to euthanise the puppy to prevent further pain and suffering. He simply could not believe it. In the end, I did euthanise the puppy. I know I felt I did the right thing but I know he did not sleep well that night, having witnessed an act he did not believe in. In this instance, it was religion and belief that caused the divide.

Another time, I had consent to perform a dental on Sidney, a 12-year-old Jack Russell Terrier. My client complained about bad breath and I could see loose teeth and extreme decay. Consent was given as written on the consent form: 'Dental under general anaesthetic and treat as indicated'. I explained that all teeth would be assessed and removed as necessary and the rest would be thoroughly cleaned (by scaling and polishing). My client seemingly agreed, signed the document and left his pet under our care. Eventually, I had to remove

12 teeth and cleaned the remaining. On discharge, my client was extremely distraught with the fact that I had removed the teeth without his 'OK'. He said that he had signed consent for the procedure, expecting me to detail to him over the phone each tooth to be removed before actually removing it. He felt like he was forced to consent the extractions he did not expect. For obvious reasons, there was no way to repair the damage in this case and a disagreement had occurred. It did not really matter who was right or wrong in this matter, just that the understanding (or misunderstanding) of a dental had occurred because the expectation of the same procedure was different and effective communication did not take place.

Past experiences –

There could have been some specific experience that changed you. It changed the way you think and act. It may have allowed you to have ideas that could be quite contrary to the 'norm'. (On this point, I challenge you to find a 'normal' person!)

Robert had a dog in the past that died under anaesthetic when performing a 'routine' spay. That incident made him extremely uncomfortable with general anaesthetics in fear of it happening again. After all, it was a conscious decision made for his completely healthy pet. When he brought his current dog, Rose, a

45kg lively Rottweiler, to me, she was three years old (he had her when she was a puppy) and had been consistently displaying aggressive behaviour during seasons to a point where he and his teenage daughter had been bitten badly. I explained (after ruling out obvious medical issues) that spaying her would be a reasonable option and potentially curative. As expected, it was an extremely difficult decision for him (compared to many pet guardians) due to his past experience. In the end (after two years when she was five years old), we did spay her uneventfully (thankfully!) which stopped the aggression and he was pleased. However, it can be seen how his past experience caused him to struggle to make certain decisions (in this case, two years were taken to obtain consent both physically and emotionally).

Unexpected cost (perception of value) –

This is one of the two most common reasons why you may fall out with your vet, the other being poor communication. Cost has traditionally been an extremely difficult topic to get right, simply because the value of veterinary care is so poorly communicated.

First of all, no one really wants to discuss the cost of medical care unless it is needed and by that time, it could well be too late anyway! When was the last time you discussed the cost of a fracture repair or a gall bladder removal with your doctor when you did not need one?!

Secondly, specifically in the UK, the presence of the NHS (National Health Service) has made the concept of medical care costs virtually non-existent. You may simply do not have any concept of how much medical care costs so when your vet presents a bill, it is always a bit of a 'shock' as you have nothing to compare with (apart from other vet bills). This is due to lack of education by medical professionals (NHS and veterinary) on the value of medicine.

More needs to be done on general education of the value of medical care for you and your pet. An immediate suggestion would be more transparency when discussing the cost of all procedures before proceeding. A difficulty lies in that sometimes costs can be unpredictable in veterinary medicine, as what exactly needs to be done may not be straight forward. It depends on what is found (during further diagnostics) or how your pet responds to the treatment (like the need to change treatment if the original method is not working). These conditions can make it challenging for your vet when discussing cost with you but certainly will need to be broached with finesse and clarity.

Disagreements can be made worse when there is no prior understanding between your vet and you. It could be the first time that your vet interacts with you when offering the options available. The consultation could range from options for bone cancer or diabetes to choice of flea treatments or vaccinations. Why you disagree does not really matter as the end result is usually a negative feeling for you and/or your vet.

- **I want to tell you what I think NOW!**

The best time to voice personal beliefs is in the beginning. Your vet should make her beliefs, expectations and intentions clear from the start (sometimes through marketing or personal communication) so you know what sort of vet she is. This allows you to make an informed decision whether this is the sort of vet that you would like to work with. You should also express your concerns, beliefs and make your expectations clear from the start to allow your vet to know if she can work with you to ensure a positive outcome.

When you are dating, you would usually find out if your values match with your date's to ensure longevity in the relationship. For example, religion, certain views, where to settle down, whether your date desires children or not, etc. These are very important questions to ensure a good fit. You know that.

However, it is almost incredulous that you may not do the same when it comes to your relationship with your vet. Perhaps, in the past, it was not needed due to the limited information, limited expectations and relatively few medical options. However, in the recent decade, with vast improvements in veterinary medicine allowing more treatment options, the use of the internet where almost any information is made accessible to you, and the increased in number of companion animals being treated as part of the family (not just a pet), the need for you to have a true relationship with your vet is becoming more obvious. It is almost a necessity to reduce the amount of disagreements due to lack of mutual understanding and increase value being imparted to your vet and you.

• Come, let's be honest and open!

Just like how a healthy relationship that is meant to thrive (not just exist), full disclosure of personal beliefs, expectations, past experiences and intention is strongly recommended. Allowances are also required for future learning and unexpected events that may occur for your vet and you.

Like a growing relationship, it should be built on a foundation of understanding, strong alignment of beliefs, mutual trust and profound respect for each other. Not only would it allow for your similarities to be celebrated, your differences would be met with compassion, appreciation and reverence as well.

Your vet may shudder at the thought of speaking her mind to you and vice versa. I believe this could partly be due to low self-esteem and the fear of rejection. You may be thinking, *What if she laughs at me? What if she thinks I am a bad pet guardian? If I do not mention it, the topic may not even appear so why go through the bother of possible embarrassment or creating probable negative feelings now?*

On the other hand, your vet may also be thinking, *What if she laughs at me? What if my qualification is questioned? What if she thinks I am being unhelpful? If I do not mention it, the topic may not even appear so why go through the bother of possible embarrassment or creating probable negative feelings now?*

Do you see the similarities? Do you see the irony?

The problem with the above thought process is the same in any relationship. If and when the topic does occur, your relationship crumbles easily as it was built on instability, fear and uncertainty. A simple disagreement may easily be magnified a thousand times in those situations.

You and your vet need to rise above these fears, overcome your low self-esteem and make deliberate relationships. It is important because in a strong relationship, more value will be imparted to your vet and you. It will also result in an immense amount of goodwill generated compared to a weak and casual relationship.

Takeaway: Varying beliefs can be encountered due to different past experiences, knowledge exposure, attitudes, racial paradigms and simply, ignorance. To enable a fruitful and long-lasting relationship between you and your vet, both parties must have mutual respect and understanding of each other's beliefs. It would be extremely simple and straightforward if beliefs were aligned. In the eventuality that they are not (which is common), at least an acknowledgement of the differences should be addressed and respected. More importantly, some form of agreement and understanding should be in place so it will not be an issue should the need arise to address it. Otherwise, your relationship may be fraught with mistrust, misunderstanding and is likely to yield a negative outcome eventually.

IF YOU DON'T LIKE SOMETHING, CHANGE IT. IF YOU CAN'T CHANGE IT, CHANGE YOUR ATTITUDE.

– Maya Angelou

In the previous chapters, we have learnt about maximising your relationship and expressing your beliefs to your vet. Next, brace yourself as I will bring insight on how your vet thinks and why she does what she does.

MY VET HAS A STRANGE BRAIN

Your Vet's Mind:

Why does she think so different

from you? Or does she?

Note: PLEASE SKIP THIS CHAPTER IF YOU HAVE NO INTEREST IN HOW A VET WAS TRAINED. You do NOT need to know this. You do NOT need to see how I made a fool of myself. You can jump straight into the next chapter.

I have been asked many times, "What do you think I should do?" I have always marvelled about the trust given by you, your pet's guardian, when you ask me this question. The fact that you are allowing me to decide what happens to your pet by giving you my opinion is extremely humbling and only pushes me to excel in my craft further.

Here, I am going to briefly describe my training as a vet and pull back the curtains on what has been taught, how I was taught and what I have learnt along the way. I certainly cannot speak for all vets for this is my personal journey. However, it will give you an idea of how a specific vet was trained.

- **Why do vets become vets?**

I remember always wanting to be a vet since the age of 10. I would rescue animals, from kittens to ducks, from hamsters to rabbits. My neighbours and family would bring animals that needed rescuing to me. I would nurse them with all I had and release them into the wild again. And pets, man, I was crazy about my pets. In my childhood, I had seven Miniature Pinschers, two pythons, one oriental whip snake, 18 terrapins, numerous mice and locusts. An innate love for animals existed in me.

My parents were not massive fans of animals (strangely) so it was hard to say the love stemmed from them. My sister is not that keen on pets either. My dad was always the joker. When his friends found out that I wanted to be a vet and asked him, "Wow, your son wants to be a vet. He must love animals. Do you like animals too?" he would promptly reply, "Of course! They are delicious!" So this marked an auspicious beginning to my vet education! Nonetheless, my entire family has been extremely supportive of my career choice and have understood more about this noble profession since then.

Speaking to my counterparts, a common thread lay where all of us love animals and wanted a career helping them. Some of my friends came from farming backgrounds, had parents who were vets or just had an innate love for animals and the desire to help them. Regardless of their background, I believe that at the core, vets want to help animals and hence, embarked on the training to do so. A strong reason is certainly needed to invest at least five years of study and dedicating the rest of your to life doing it!

- **Vetwarts – A Place of Magic Potions and Marvellous Experimentations**

From the first day at the Royal Veterinary College (RVC), we were taught that 20% of the problems lay with the animals and 80% with the guardians and that solving the animal's condition (diagnosis and treatment) is relatively easy compared to solving the guardian's concerns. How true is that! On the other hand, how is it possible that the time and syllabus spent on the education to be a vet did not reflect these needs?!

As vet graduates, we are far better equipped to deal with the medical conditions of the animal species compared to the understanding of the psychological and emotional needs of you, your pet's guardian. We were simply not taught and had to rely on our 'natural' instinct (which is not natural at all!), our 'gut feel' (depends on your gut!) and finally, 'common sense' (hard to apply common sense considering you are unique and your pets have unique circumstances!) to navigate your exclusively complex mind!

- ## Royal Veterinary College – the BEST college there is

Studying in London was one of the best times of my life. It was then I learnt a lot about myself. Imagine coming straight from a tiny island city like Singapore after completing your National Service. It was an extremely foreign (pardon the pun!) experience, attending university in London. Due to the strong pound, life was always on a shoestring budget. It usually is tight for a student anyway, especially in London, but the additional strain of paying full tuition fees using a weaker currency was incredibly challenging. Thinking outside the box and resilience were necessary to enhance living in happiness. Apart from studying full-time, having two to three jobs on the side, earning money to pay for accommodation and life was unavoidable.

Being in the RVC was a wonderful experience. Her lecturers were so passionate in their expertise and sharing the knowledge with her students. Lessons were filled with so much information (not all relevant, of course) and I was clearly fascinated. My classmates were made up of some of the best people on the planet. They welcomed me the best they could despite my unfamiliar culture and accent. The idea of teaching veterinary medicine is a daunting one. I have huge admiration for anyone who comes up with a syllabus designed to present veterinary medicine to a student. To be able to slowly build up the basic knowledge, the bare foundation for someone, before putting on layers of complexity in various areas of studies until succeeding in sharing the entire knowledge to literally convert a layperson into a vet in five years is just incredible. Sure, there are some who will always criticise that lessons could be taught better, the structure of the course could be improved and complain that things could be made easier or more logical. I challenge those who think like that to create their own syllabus and run their own course. I believe that if we are open, we are able to absorb lessons regardless of shape or form, own it and make it ours. Certainly things have to move with the times and lesson structure can be modified but I believe we should be grateful for all that is provided. RVC has done and is still continuing to do an exceptional job.

- **Baby Steps**

The first two preclinical years of this five-year course were carried out at the RVC Camden Campus. I was living in Russell Square and walked to college daily. They consisted of subjects like cell biology, ethics, biochemistry, physiology (how things work), anatomy (name and location of body parts) and plenty of extra-mural studies (studying outside college, EMS for short).

We had plenty of lectures that ranged from fascinating and engaging to downright dry and extremely hard to get interested in. It largely depended on the topic and the lecturer! One of my favourite lectures was when our bovine (cow) lecturer, Dr Martin Sheldon, was writhing around the stage showing us how a calf is born! It was epic! Tutorial sessions after lectures to allow discussions were held daily. Presenting your research was expected. It was at this moment in time when I learnt that my grasp of English was not as good as I thought it would be!

When I first came to the UK from Singapore, I was a young man fresh out of the military (compulsory National Service in Singapore), hot blooded and brash (being an officer instructor can instil a certain a degree of false sense of confidence in you!). In the first term, a debate on the topic of euthanasia and overtreatment was being held in Ethics. I was elected to present our team's point of view. It was really hard to say whether it was because they needed a sacrificial lamb or I appeared to be game for anything.

Nonetheless, I gave a 10-minute presentation to 40 bright minds in class. I spoke confidently and purposefully, displaying all the presentation techniques I have acquired in my military leadership course and delivered the points that had been discussed in the past hour. I could feel the room being quiet and still, hanging onto my every word. Thoughtful glances were riveted on me. *I got them!* I thought. *I am invincible!* I was feeling good. I was feeling high. *This is how it is done,* I thought to myself.

So imagine my horror and embarrassment when I sat down and nudged my teammate beside me and asked, "So, what do you think about that?"

She replied, "Sorry, Lennon, I had no idea what you just said. I did not understand a single word!"

In my mind, I was articulating with finesse. The reality was that no one understood my heavy Singapore accent, especially with the incredible speed which I spoke with (normal for Singaporeans to speak fast!). I was aghast and mortified! I wanted to hide under the table and leave the room at the same time (I was not sure which was better!).

The worst part was, our point still needed to be made! So, my friend, Matt, had to take up the challenge and present the same speech again but in a much more readily-understood Welsh accent. The horror! My friends, even up to now, tell me that was one of the funniest things they had experienced. I see the humour in it but it is really tough when you are the star in the comedy!

The anatomy sessions were held in the basement laboratory. It often reeked of the formalin that was used to preserve the cadavers that were being dissected. Teams of four to five would share a table and a cadaver (animal corpse). So, each table would usually receive an entire animal (dog for example). Depending on which anatomy was being studied, the body system of interest would be removed and the rest of the cadaver returned to the chiller. By the time the last body system was being examined weeks later, the smell would be getting very pungent. The funny thing is, dissection classes are usually held just before lunch and (please do not ask me why!) often stimulated hunger pangs. I am aware it sounds morbid and weird but it is true. Vets are indeed strange creatures...

Extra-mural studies in the preclinical years consisted of a few weeks of lambing, a couple of weeks working with cows and pigs each, a couple of weeks working with horses and a few weeks to choose any species. I loved my EMS! Reports had to be submitted after completion. I remember my lambing experience fondly. I was on a farm in the depth of Wales, near Cowbridge. Bearing in mind that I had merely spent less than six months out of Singapore and the only concept of sheep I had having lived in Singapore City all my life was 'Baa Baa Black

Sheep' and 'Mary Had A Little Lamb', working on a sheep farm was fairly surreal! Before long, I was lambing like a veteran! Friends in Singapore just could not comprehend what I was doing.

- **Getting Real**

The last three clinical years at RVC were held at Hawkshead Campus in Potters Bar, just outside North London. Just like we had spent our pre-clinical years learning normal anatomy and physiology of the animal species, now we learned about the things that can go wrong. Just like before, lessons comprised of lectures and small group learning.

It was extremely challenging living in the suburbs after being in Singapore and London. It was a beautiful campus but it was solely filled with veterinary people! I sought solace and sanity by travelling into London almost every weekend for sports and to see non-vet friends.

During this time, we spent a lot of time 'seeing practice' at various vet practices. It was probably the closest thing we had that was most useful as it allowed us to actually experience life after graduation and to have a glimpse of what we were going to be doing as qualified vets. This was when I realised that the variation of vet practices was as vast as the different countries in the world. No practice was the same. The standards, protocols, personnel, customers, equipment used and culture differed greatly. It was mind boggling how a profession could differ so much. I have seen no less than seven different techniques to neuter a cat, countless protocols for treating similar diseases, various approaches to diagnosing the same condition and multiple communication methods. In fact, the only thing that varied the least was the animals.

On farms, both beef cattle and dairy cows were raised differently therefore requiring different vet inputs and management. Horses were kept for a variety of reasons and hence each consultation was modified to the need of the guardian. As for companion pets, the variation of vet practices and what they did was so diverse that it was difficult to believe we were still in the same profession!

For example, in some practices, I saw the 'standard' treatment for any sick pet was a course of antibiotics and pain relief and it was only when it did not resolve that further investigations took place, whereas at other practices, investigations are conducted for a diagnosis before any treatment is advised. Certainly, I am not judging which approach is better, just observing that huge variations exist. I found it incredible that they all had the same degree, yet the outcome of the service provided was so different.

The final year was made up of clinical rotation where we spent two to four weeks experiencing a specific vocation of vet medicine like internal medicine, surgery, farm animals, anaesthesia, etc.

Finally, we each had to deep dive into a topic a chosen topic for three months. I chose anaesthesia as I was fascinated by its application across all species.

- **Into the Wild**

I started my first job in Newton Abbot. It was a mixed practice which meant that apart from pets, we looked after farm animals and horses too. It was a steep learning curve. I had amazing mentors who helped me so much when I started out. I have so much respect for them in what they did. They were patient with me when I panicked like any graduate would do. They were extremely supportive and I was lucky to have them.

For the first six months, I felt like an imposter. I was almost astounded that pet guardians were listening to my advice, much less paying for it. It was almost like an out-of-body experience. I could virtually see myself on the side performing a clinical examination and advising the guardian. It was weird. In retrospect, most of the advice I gave was sound and the results of my vetting was as expected. My training kicked in and all was fine. I have learnt that that is a common feeling most newly qualified vets have.

I was starving for knowledge. I learnt that though I had finished five years of university, my education was just about to begin. There were so many things that university did not prepare me for. Like pet guardian communication, common diseases, finances, common sense and many more. I lapped it up like a fat kid on a cupcake. I lived above the practice which made it extremely handy for me to volunteer my time for any emergency that occurred downstairs. I loved it. I immersed myself in it. I read almost every night, reviewing the cases that I saw in the day and learnt more about them, how to improve my technique, etc. I volunteered for jobs that no one else wanted to do, visiting inaccessible farms, seeing difficult customers and doing extra hours and oncalls just to learn more. I found out that is common practice for enthusiastic learners.

Over time, I slowly and quietly grew confident in my skills and knowledge. I validated myself with the results of my patients. When they got better and the guardians were happy, I felt accomplished.

It was not all smooth sailing of course. There was a bitch spay that I performed that was seen as an out-of-hours consultation at 11pm with one guardian holding her dog and her husband holding her intestines. The suture holding everything in place had come undone and her intestines literally fell out when she jumped up on the couch. I assisted the surgeon to pack the intestines back and treated the infection that occurred. After two other midline exlaps (opening her belly up and closing it after), she finally showed signs of recovery after eight days. This happened six months into the job.

I was mortified. I had to question myself on my competency of being a vet. I could not operate for the next two weeks. Though the dog survived and the (amazing) guardians were extremely understanding and supportive, I still felt like a failure and that I did not have the skills to be a vet and had chosen the wrong trade. Initially, it took me weeks to regain confidence to operate again and probably two years before I truly believed in myself. Sometimes, you may not see or understand what your vet goes through treating your animal, the responsibility that your vet takes on personally and the effects of doing something wrong have on her. You may think that it is just a number and she will get over it. The reality is, from what I gather from other vets and my personal experience, your vet will take it extremely personally and certainly may not get over it that fast. I believe that your vet does care deeply and strives to do her best all the time.

I will always be grateful for my first job where I was supported by an amazing team, some of whom I am still great friends with today.

- **I want to learn more!**

Like many of my counterparts, I dedicated my next few years to honing my veterinary interests and skills. I chose jobs that I felt would further my career and understanding, stayed as long as I was still learning and left when I found another place that would expand my journey.

Subsequently, I accepted my second job that allowed me to spend a day volunteering at the local zoo's vet department as it was something I had always wanted to do. After spending a day weekly for 18 months, I learnt so much regarding wildlife. I helped in a 350kg gorilla's general anaesthetic, assisted in amputating a toe of a red river hog, vaccinated 30lb tiger cubs (they are so cute but so feisty! Imagine a ball of striped spitfire!), observed countless post mortems including a giraffe's (so sad but fascinating at the same time!) and so many experiences that would never been seen otherwise and for that, I am eternally grateful. However, during these times, I realised that I was never going to be a zoo vet as I was not ready to accept the full implications. At the same time, I also pursued my interest in veterinary acupuncture which led me to my third job as it was not supported in the practice I was in.

My boss, Dr Phil Davies, in my third job was instrumental in pushing me out of my comfort zone by suggesting and supporting that I started an additional qualification in internal medicine. With the support of the practice and a lot of time on my part, I spent the next two years studying for my certificate and completing it. It increased my knowledge and boosted the level of my game tenfold. I was able to diagnose better, treat better and achieve better clinical outcomes for my patients. I felt amazing, having the power to create effective positive change. You may not realise that your vet's knowledge is unique and her consultation may differ from others. Shortly after, I also studied keyhole surgery.

I then moved on to another, bigger vet practice to manage a branch surgery. This exposed my management skills or rather, the lack of it. On top of vetting, I was writing rotas, conducting staff appraisals, managing my team and learning more about the financial aspects. It was indeed a steep learning curve.

Finally, I took the plunge and did what I always wanted to do since graduation. I founded Amity Veterinary Care in Newton Abbot, UK.

- **They didn't teach me that at Vet College!**

The lessons I have learnt from working can be credited to four sources.

The first source is myself. I studied the topics I was naturally interested in like surgery, exotic medicine, acupuncture and minimally invasive (keyhole) surgery. I took courses, attended meetings, went through my patients' cases I saw in the day and read books at night. The source was innate. I chose what I wanted to read. The advantage was that it was easy to read as I selected what I wanted to study. The growth was good but finite as I was limited to my own imagination.

The second source is my work place. Experienced clinicians, vet nurses and support teams like the practice manager and receptionists provided a plethora of working life experience. They gave tremendous support and I learnt a lot about practice management, teamwork, understanding the various roles each team member played and how the practice flowed as a business (and a single entity) to enable veterinary work to be conducted.

The third source of my education is from the animals. Every single animal I have treated is unique. It could be a cat, a dog or a bird, they are never the same. They each have their own specific quirks, behaviour and attitudes. Even their anatomy differs slightly despite being the same species (no two Persians are the same!). They fill me with a sense of awe with their presence. They taught me about companionship with their pet guardians. The power that they yield, the satisfaction and grief they provide for their guardians. They remind me of the beauty of nature and all of God's amazing creation. I feel honoured to be in a position to help them.

The last source of my learning comes from you, your wonderful pet's guardian. You provide the deepest, most sought after, greatest and the most difficult lessons in the entire profession. Arguably, the treatments for the conditions of animals do not differ much. For example, the treatment for a cat with diabetes is limited to only so many options, mostly involving insulin and diet management. However, every bond between your pet and you is unique. It requires deep understanding of your beliefs, expectations, past experiences and personal situation to allow me to prescribe the best treatment plan for your pet. It is from you that I learn how to communicate my ideas, feel empathy, conduct the most effective consultation and in doing so, gain self-knowledge. Yes, from you, I learn more about myself. Veterinary medicine is more than just treating animals. To me, it is more about preserving the bond between your pet and you. To solely treat your pet medically is not enough. I need to understand your pet's guardian as well and only you can provide that knowledge.

- **Deconstructing a Vet Consultation**

Here, I am going to explain the structure of a veterinary consultation. It is a four-part structure that has been taught in university and one many vets adopt in UK.

The first part of the consultation comprises understanding the problem of your pet. Your vet would learn about your pet's medical history by reading his current notes or notes from his previous vets. This would allow her to understand any medical issues which may be relevant like drug allergies, past similar conditions that have occurred, etc. She would then address the current issues. She might delve into the specifics of the problem. For example, if your pet is lame, questions may include how long has he been lame for, any event that could have brought about the lameness, whether it is improving or deteriorating, etc. She can assess the severity and understand the condition better. She may also find out how you are being affected by this problem by simply asking, "How is this problem affecting you?" This allows her to address your deeper problems and express empathy and understanding on top of helping your pet.

The second part of the consultation is the clinical examination. Your vet may start by observing your pet from a distance. This allows assessment to be made without the interference of animal handling. Hands-on examination usually follows. Frequently, your vet would examine your pet entirely from the front to the back (nose-to-tail approach). This allows nothing else to be missed out. It is not uncommon to leave the affected area until last. For example, if your pet is limping on his right front leg, your vet may choose to thoroughly examine that leg last. Additional tests may be carried out, for example, x-rays, if she feels it is necessary.

The third part is where your vet will tell you what is happening. Sometimes, it may be obvious what the problem is, like an infected nail bed or a simple fracture. Other times, it may not be straight forward, for example, having several possible conditions that causes your pet to drink and urinate more than usual.

The last part of the consultation comprises of either helping your pet if the diagnosis is known or further investigations to find out more. Sometimes the latter is crucial to ensure the right treatment is given and not make things worse. This is when your concerns are addressed, not just your pet's. Treatment usually involves medication, surgery, management or simply monitoring. It could also be a combination of above.

- **If I want to find out more, I need to...**

As much as your vet would love to arrive to the exact diagnosis on clinical examination, sometimes it is not possible and further diagnostics may be suggested. It may be performing radiographs (taking x-rays), blood testing, sampling a lump to look under a microscope and many various tests. I have tried the crystal ball which was purchased from Amazon (and Argos) but unfortunately, it just was not that useful!

Usually, the purpose of further diagnostics is to find out more about the condition *and* hence decide what treatment option should be taken. It can be argued that if a decision has been made to exclude a treatment option already, it may be pointless to perform further testing apart from acquiring knowledge. For example, if there was a mass found on your pet and you have decided (for various reasons) not to treat at all, it may be pointless to find out what the mass was as it does not change the outcome for your pet unless you only wanted to know what the mass was.

You may get frustrated when your vet recommends further testing as it may not appear to be necessary and potentially incurring more cost. This is where the trust and mutual understanding between your vet and you is paramount as it all comes down to just that. Do you trust your vet's expertise, integrity and her understanding of you to believe her advice is accurate and given in the best interest for your pet and you?

It is more probable that you tend to doubt the suggested tests due to the mistrust of your vet rather than the test itself. It is important for your vet to explain the reason behind the decision of suggesting the test. Pros and cons should be explained and weighed for you such that you can make an informed decision.

Once further testing has taken place and a diagnosis has been made, a more specific and useful treatment plan can be recommended and a more accurate prognosis can be given.

• Let's give it some Magic Potion

Once a diagnosis (provisional or confirmed) has been made, consideration will be taken to prescribe and dispense the medication that will help your pet. It is interesting to point out that your vet belongs to the only medical profession that is allowed to prescribe and dispense at the same time and location. If you were to visit your doctor, they would write a prescription and you would obtain your medication from a dispensary, not from them.

This means that your vet has an additional requirement compared to your doctor, to have suitable areas where medicines are kept. These medicines need to be kept at certain temperatures (either in the room or in the fridge) where daily readings are recorded. Some medicines are restricted, potentially dangerous and need to be kept in a locked metal cupboard. All these systems are regulated, incurring effort and cost to maintain them.

There is a protocol that your vet follows to prescribe medication. It is known as 'the cascade'. Basically, your vet needs to exercise responsibility when choosing what drugs to prescribe. The cascade is as follows...

1. Vets need to use a licensed medicine if it exists for that said species and condition.

2. If there is no such medicine, then a medicine used for the same species for another condition or for a different species for the same condition can be used.

3. If there is no such medicine, then a human drug or a specially formulated drug can be used.

She has to weigh the pros and cons of each medication and perform a risk/benefit analysis for all treatments. Sometimes, it is done quickly due to familiarity and experience, sometimes extra attention needs to be paid if it involves a complicated medicine, a complicated protocol or for an unfamiliar species. Either way, the pros and cons should be discussed with you, so you can make an informed decision and all risks are made known and accepted.

The choice of formulation of the drug is also important. For example, it is more useful to use an injection if you struggle giving tablets. Sometimes, choosing a medication that needs to be given once a month may be more convenient than giving daily.

Different conditions will require different lengths of medication. For example, it is not uncommon that antibiotic treatment for skin infection can last from three to eight weeks depending on the severity. Some conditions will require lifelong medication if the intention is management, not cure. For example, heart or arthritic medication. It is not uncommon for your vet to monitor your pet closely in these cases to make sure that it is still safe to continue the medicine. These may include clinical examinations, blood testing or urine testing at regular intervals.

- **Under the Blade and Playing God**

Some conditions require surgery to solve the problem. It is not treatable with medical management and a scalpel is involved.

Elective (by choice) procedures would include neutering and non-elective (no choice) procedures would include amputation, fixing fractures and other procedures that would improve the quality of life of your pet.

Some seemingly 'routine' or 'common' procedures can be technically difficult. For example, the open bitch spay still causes some experienced vets to feel a chill down their spine, sweat a bit more and feel stressed before the procedure.

Some surgical procedures are considered advanced and may receive a better outcome when performed by an experienced vet who has advanced knowledge (for example, a specialist).

In the UK, apart from straight forward and quick procedures, like placing a couple of staples on a clean wound or lancing an abscess on the thinnest part of the skin, most vets would agree that at least sedation or a full general anaesthetic is required before performing surgery.

A concern that you and your vet share (though perhaps to a lesser extent due to more understanding and knowledge) is general anaesthetic risk. A scientific study led by Dr Brodbelt, a British, board-certified anaesthesiologist, showed that the death rate under sedation or anaesthesia is around 0.15% on average. Meaning 99.85% of patients survive anaesthesia and sedation, clearly an overwhelming majority. This research is exceptional as 98,000 dogs participated, an unusually large sample for a veterinary study. The average age of the dogs was eight years old and the anaesthesia lasted for an average of one hour, for a variety of procedures performed by general practitioners as well as specialists.

As expected, the anaesthesia risks increased with sick, older (over 12 years old), smaller (under 4kg) and certain breeds of dogs. The risks were also went up when more involved procedures had taken place.

The general anaesthetic risk for cats is similar to dogs.

The general anaesthetic risk for exotic species may be slightly higher.

Before your vet would suggest surgery as a treatment (or part of a treatment) to you, the factors she would usually consider are her (or someone else's) competency for the procedure and general anaesthetic risk for your pet. These are important conversations that are crucial in managing expectations.

• **Test and Measure**

Once a confirmed diagnosis (or provisional diagnoses) has been made, your vet would suggest a treatment plan or more often, a few options. Most, if not all, treatment options have pros and cons. Some pros include fast recovery to normal health, most effective method to solve a problem, cost effective, easy to administer and simple. Some cons include higher cost, high failure rate, complicated to administer, higher degree of invasiveness to your pet and involving a sedative/general anaesthetic.

Usually, your vet would explain the different options for your pet's condition with their associated pros/cons to you. It is important that you understand the advantages and disadvantages to enable an informed decision to be made. Every pet guardian is different. Your expectations, financial situation, beliefs and views for what is good for you and your pet can differ greatly from others and that is OK! There really isn't a right or wrong answer as long as the decision is informed.

Once you have made your decision for your pet's treatment, it is common practice for your vet to recommend a re-examination to make sure the treatment is working and your pet is improving. For example, if your pet had diarrhoea and lost weight, your vet would check, after treatment, if the diarrhoea had resolved and his weight had maintained or increased. After all, she cannot improve what she does not measure. There are times when you may wish for peace of mind, having your vet check your pet over and giving him a clean bill of health.

The timing for the re-examination can differ depending

on the situation. For example, an eye ulcer may be re-examined after a few days of treatment as it is important to make sure the eye (being such a precious and delicate structure) is responding well to treatment and change the approach rapidly if the original treatment is ineffective. On the other hand, antibiotics take longer to work so the re-examination may not take place for at least a week (or longer).

• You don't understand what I want!

When I first qualified, I applied my Vet College education and used my expertise in treating the animals the best way I knew how. I was working in the day and revising case studies at night. I was learning the science of recognising the symptoms you told me your pet was showing, honing my clinical examination and presenting all the treatment options.

It was only after a few years (yes, I am a slow learner!), I began to understand that my job also included you, not just focusing on your pet. I began to tailor my consultation to include you, listening more intently, catching the mild nuances that may not be obvious but extremely important to you. I began to understand you more and learnt that my role is not only treating your pet but also helping you in a very big way.

I learnt that I was in a position to make a huge impact on not only your pet's life but also yours. I began to listen and understand your wishes, beliefs, expectations and appreciating that there could be circumstances that will affect the treatment options and to know them would greatly improve how you feel.

The role of your vet is to bridge the science of animal healing with your wishes and expectations using her medical knowledge and human emotional intelligence without compromise of her duty to your pet and also your beliefs. It can indeed be a tricky job at times, not unlike walking on a tightrope, keeping balance in all directions without falling and yet still proceeding in the right direction. Veterinary medicine should not be simply medical.

Only by taking time to listen and truly understand you, is your vet able to give the best advice beyond just treating your pet, but build trust between you which ultimately allows the bond between your pet and you to be maintained or even improved.

• Show me the Proof!

You may have heard your vet mention the term 'Evidence based veterinary medicine' (EBVM). This came into UK veterinary medicine after the millennium. It combines clinical expertise, the most relevant and best available scientific evidence, your pet's circumstances and your values. Even though it may seem that every veterinary decision is based on evidence, in reality, it may not be as easy or straightforward as it sounds.

The challenges include:

➢ Information available is often spread over many sources and vets do not have time or resources to seek them out

➢ Time being limited to analyse the evidence at that moment when treating your pet

➢ Uncertainty in determining the validity and independent nature of the studies, especially when funded by commercial organisations

➢ Actual lack of information

➢ Your expectations, beliefs and desires may differ from EBVM

Ideally, all veterinary decisions should be made on known protocols but it is not often possible due to the reasons above. Instead, your vet usually uses the best of her knowledge to provide advice and treatment suggestions.

• Never straight-forward!

As such, all veterinary decisions are usually biased (albeit extremely subtle in cases) due to different personal experiences and the expertise of your vet. Factors like locality may come into play as well. For example, the suspicion for lungworm infection may be higher in areas where lungworm infections are more common.

Due to the training and personal beliefs of your vet, it may affect how she approaches a case. This may show in the way she obtains the medical history, the way she performs the clinical examination, the range of possible diagnoses she offers and finally, the treatment options either in further investigations or treatment plans she suggests.

This is where your thoughts, beliefs and expectations really matter. Do make them known to your vet as it will help her to make better suggestions for you.

- **It is an opinion in the end**

Ultimately, despite what any one may say, evidence based or not, you should understand that it is an opinion in the end. It should not be surprising as that can be said in pretty much all professions. For example, hairdressing, law, education, retail, plumbing, health food shops, etc. The ultimate decision made by a professional (or an expert) in the end is but an opinion.

- **Vets' pets**

Have you ever wondered what your vet's pet is like? As vets are professionally trained, are their pets usually kept healthy? Do all vets treat their pets as soon as they can so the problem is nipped in the bud? Do vets have healthy pets in general? Do vets practice what they preach? Do you expect a doctor to be healthy, a mechanic to have a problem-free car or a builder to have a completely functional house?

Let me share with you my insight on vets' pets...

Cleo is a five-year-old black and white domestic short-haired cat belonging to Natalie, a skin specialist. Cleo has no less than four different skin conditions, of which one is extremely rare and has strange symptoms.

Mavis is an eight-year-old female entire (not spayed) greyhound belonging to Liz, an experienced vet. Liz enjoys the difference in temperament when Mavis comes into season so has decided not to spay her. If a pyometra (infected womb) should occur, she would spay her then.

Gonzales is a well-loved ten-year-old male bunny that is owned by an exotic species specialist, Patricia. He has only three legs due to an unfortunate accident. I remember having long conversations with Patricia regarding his quality of life. It is interesting how it can be so difficult to have an objective view on your own pet.

Before I studied to be a vet, I worked at a vet practice in Singapore as an Assistant. There were three dogs and 15 cats that the vet (also the owner) had accumulated (rescued) over the years. There was Snowy, a seven-year-old overweight Golden Retriever that was abandoned by her guardians. Her resting place was under the reception counter by my feet. Girl-girl was a five-year-old feisty Pomeranian that would snap your fingers off if she felt like it. Her resting haven was ON the reception table! Last but not least, Oscar was a 12-year-old pug with chronic skin disease. He was also abandoned by his guardians as they could not afford the time or money to manage his skin.

Then, there were the 15 resident cats that needed feeding and cleaning daily. These cats would have lived at the practice till their end of days.

Personally, I have had multiple pets in the past. Some I have kept very well and others, perhaps the husbandry could be improved. What I am trying to impress is that your vet is just like you, faced with the same responsibilities, trials and tribulations of caring for a pet. Pets are not absent of problems just because they are cared for by a vet. Sometimes, your level of care for your pet may be higher than your vet's. Sometimes, your vet also struggles with her pets like you. Occasionally, your vet may also make bad judgement calls or mistakes with her pets.

Your vet would be learning all the time from her pet and be constantly taught lessons that are not covered in university.

Takeaway: As you may appreciate, there are multitudes of factors that can affect your vet's journey in learning, leading to the final action of presenting the choice of treatment options for your pet. Every vet and her journey is unique. That is why it is impossible to make an opinion on all vets based on your one experience. Similar to you, not all vets are the same. Though your vet's intentions may be perfect, her execution may be flawed. In the end, she merely wants the best outcome for your pet and you. Your vet is only able to provide the best advice with what she knows. So perhaps, if you ask your vet, "How do you think and give advice?" she would probably reply, "I will use all my knowledge and everything in my power to provide the best advice for you." I suspect all vets do.

IT IS WHAT YOU LEARN AFTER YOU THINK YOU KNOW EVERYTHING THAT MATTERS.

– Anonymous

After learning about how a vet is trained in the UK, we will look at alternative medicine/food and vets' attitudes toward them.

VETS KNOW IT ALL. OR DO THEY?

Medicine not taught at Vet College (Bonus on raw feeding)

Maisy is a beautiful, doe-eyed, nine-year-old female Basset Hound that I see regularly for acupuncture. After the first session, she would lovingly rub her back towards me when I saw her as if saying, "Stick needles in me here and now! It makes me feel so good!" Maisy benefits greatly from acupuncture. Her guardian reports an increased ease of movement, playfulness and happiness.

Within the veterinary industry, there has been an extreme rift formed between some vets that practise and support treatments that are not 'conventionally' taught in vet schools and other vets who vehemently declare the uselessness of them and even proclaim them as harmful. Such treatments are known as 'alternative', 'complementary', 'holistic' and 'integrative' veterinary medicine. The fact that these four extremely different terms are used interchangeably demonstrates the lack of understanding of the entire idea and philosophy behind it.

In this chapter, we will investigate the views of pet guardians and vets on this topic. To conclude, we will suggest a few tips to enable your vet to work with you in this area. A bonus topic on raw feeding is included.

- **What's the difference?**

"Alternative" is defined as 'available as another possibility or choice' or 'activities that depart from or challenge traditional norms'.

"Complementary" is defined as 'combining in such a way as to enhance or emphasise the qualities of each other or another'.

Taking a "holistic" approach is characterised by treating the whole living animal, taking into account mental and social factors, rather than just the symptoms of a disease.

"Integrative" is combining two or more things to form an effective unit or system.

Many vets who practice and/or support medicine not taught in depth at Vet College like acupuncture, physiotherapy, hydrotherapy and laser therapy usually refer to these approaches as complementary and/or integrative. They usually believe each method and approach has its merits and limitations. Thus by combining them, a desired outcome can be produced.

There are some professionals who solely practice methods that they consider to replace 'conventional' medicine or are used when 'conventional' medicine has failed. These professionals usually refer to what they practise as alternative. It includes (not exclusively!) homeopathy, herbal medicine and reiki. The approach and understanding to address the condition is vastly different such that it is not easy to combine the treatments. It is like choosing a Mac or a PC. Both camps have their strong beliefs and yet solve similar problems.

There are a few practitioners that integrate all disciplines but they are usually extremely rare.

A common error occurs when one thinks 'holistic' means using treatment that is not 'conventional' treatment. What it really means is that apart from treating only the symptoms of the condition, other factors that may be contributing will be considered as well. For example, Troy is an old arthritic dog. Apart from just giving essential pain relief, his vet may adopt a holistic approach making sure he is of good body condition and not too fat, avoids steps, receives extra help into the car, advising his guardians to create non-slip areas where he walks and other measures that would aid his condition. It does not necessarily mean that acupuncture or other methods listed above may be used.

Understanding the differences may allow you to appreciate these methods better and improve your ability to discuss them with your vet.

- ## So many types of therapy (not exhaustive!)

In this section, we will explore the types of medicine and techniques that are not taught in depth at Vet College. It is not meant to be comprehensive for each one would be a book (or books) on its own. It is just to provide a basic understanding of each technique.

Acupuncture – Originating from China, it usually involves inserting needles at specific locations to restore balance and health to your pet. It can be used for a variety of conditions.

Homeopathy – Originating from Germany, its basic principle is that "like cures like". In other words, a substance taken in small amounts will cure the same symptoms it causes if taken in large amounts. It can be used for a variety of conditions.

T Touch – Originating from Canada, it uses a combination of circular touches, movement exercises, lifts and body wraps that allows your pet to think instead of react, and addresses issues. This technique improves body awareness and posture.

Bowen – Originating from Australia, it is a gentle therapy that is applied to areas of the body using thumbs and fingers in a specific order. It can be used to treat musculoskeletal or related neurological problems including acute sports injuries and chronic conditions.

Herbal medicine – Dating back at least 6,000 years, the use of herbs in medicine has been widespread with varying degrees. Many modern medicines are derived from herbs. Its usage is possibly only limited by our imagination.

Chiropractic – Originating from Iowa, USA, it is the practice of spinal manipulation and manual therapy. In the last decade, it has been used in animals. Controversy regarding its use is still present.

Reiki – Originating from Japan, 'Rei' means Universal Life and 'ki' means energy. It works by a transfer of energy from the hands of the Reiki Master to the affected parts of the body. It can be used for a variety of conditions.

Bach Flower Remedy – Originating from England, it is made out of watered-down extracts from the *flowers* of wild plants. It can be used for a variety of conditions.

Physiotherapy – Veterinary physiotherapists help pets affected by injury, illness or disability through movement, exercise and manual manipulations to regain their original function.

Hydrotherapy – It is a therapeutic whole-body treatment that involves moving and exercising in water; essentially physiotherapy in a pool. Water treadmills have been widely used as well. It allows your pet's limbs to be exercised with reduced weight as water supports him. It is usually used for any condition that will benefit from movement with its weight reduced like post-operative surgery and/or osteoarthritis.

Laser – It uses focused light on affected areas to induce healing at a cellular level. Class III and Class IV (more powerful) lasers are commonly used. It is usually used for pain relief and tissue healing.

- **You cannot recommend what you don't know about**

These above-mentioned techniques are not taught in depth at Vet Colleges. Unless your vet has undertaken further studies to learn about them, she probably would not have too much knowledge about them. Imagine if someone asked you an opinion on something you do not really know about, would you be able to advise with confidence, especially if it involves the health of their pet? Let me tell you a secret, one that everyone knows but is afraid to admit... VETS DO NOT KNOW EVERYTHING! Your vet wants to do the best for you and your pet and they extend all they know WITHIN THEIR KNOWLEDGE BASE. So if they are not completely sure of the methods, results and outcomes, they may hesitate in giving advice because they are being extremely responsible and want the best for your pet! I know it sounds ironic and contradictory but it is true.

In addition, there have been cases where pets have gotten worse when those treatments have failed to produce the desired results. At times, it could be based on misdiagnosis of the condition or the treatment simply isn't enough. More worryingly, there are situations where conventional treatment has been withheld due to some person's (could be a pet guardian and/or a professional) belief, resulting in the pet's condition worsening.

Certainly, as veterinary medicine remains to be a fairly scientific topic, the lack of robust evidence plays a strong role in the reluctance of recommending or implementing these methods. We know that we see the world with filters. What appears to be 'robust evidence' can be considered 'hocus pocus' to another.

• Let me show you a trick or two!

Your understanding of these various techniques may surpass your vet simply because you may have had more access to them than her. It could be that you are a practitioner yourself, you have had successful treatments in the past, you know someone who does it or you have simply found out more from others and Dr Google. It can be quite frustrating if your vet does not listen or support you and your pet.

Here are some tips to improve the likelihood of your vet supporting you or least maintaining the great relationship between you and her.

1. First of all, finding a vet who is sympathetic, open-minded and supportive about these therapies can be a great place to start! Or at least, one that does not harbour an obvious negative bias to them. You can find this out (sometimes) on the practice website, the vet's bio and by just simply asking your vet when you meet her.

2. Having a trusted relationship with your vet helps immensely in your credibility. So build that important relationship as soon as you can. The more she knows you, the more she will listen. (It works both ways, the more you know your vet, the more you will trust her!)

3. Providing scientific evidence like books and research papers may help. Vets are trained scientifically and many tend to base their decisions on proven knowledge. It gives them a better grounding for their choices.

4. Explaining the reasoning behind why you decided on that technique can help her to sympathise. For example, if you had a similar treatment that was successful or you are a practitioner yourself.

5. If you know someone specifically, it would help to give that contact to your vet as well. Sometimes, it is not because your vet do not want to support you, it could be that she does not actually know

what to do or who to go to even if she wants to help. Giving her someone you have researched and chosen may help her immensely to give permission and support.

Remember that your vet is trying to give her best advice based on the knowledge she has. She cares deeply for you and your pet. It is nothing personal. You are your pet's guardian and you know (or will know!) your pet best. Be confident and use your vet to achieve the best for your pet and you, regardless of method used.

- **Argh, it's RAW!**

Since started in 1993 (BARF) in Australia, feeding raw diets is slowly gaining popularity. Having said that, it accounts only for < 1% of the dog food trade. There are different types of raw food, for example, Biological Appropriate Raw Food (BARF), the prey model and Raw Meat Based Diet (RMBD).

All three methods involve feeding raw animal parts. It claims feeding a diet that is deemed more natural possesses health benefits for your pet. Many guardians have said that it has vastly improved their pets' lives.

One controversy lies in the increased risk of bacterial infections (for example, Salmonellosis, Campylobacter) for your pet and you as handling raw food is involved. In my experience, this is usually caused by poor hygiene and inferior product quality.

Anna knew her vet was against raw feeding (due to her vet's own admission). So when asked regarding the diet of her dog, she invariably lied and named a leading dry kibble brand. The issue laid in that she could never remember which brand she said before so gave several brands over time. As a result, her vet thinks she changes dog food often, possibly causing issues to her pet when the reality is she has only been feeding one diet, the raw diet. This leads to, at best, mistrust and confusion and at worst, misdiagnosis and mistreatment. That is mad! No one benefits.

Nutrition, much less raw feeding, is not taught in depth at Vet College. Just like humans, all dogs differ and hence their dietary requirements can differ as well. You can almost imagine (and possibly appreciate) why your vet may get concerned if she had been trained to look out for and reduce the risk of bacterial infections for your pet. She is only concerned because she cares. She may have seen the effects of Campylobacter and Salmonella causing pets to be very ill (I know I have!) and does not wish to see your pet suffer.

Presuming you practise great hygiene, obtain great quality raw food and want to try or have seen the benefits of raw feeding for your dog, how do you tell your vet so she is on your side? Here are a few tips to increase the chances of a positive outcome.

1. First of all, finding a vet who is sympathetic, open minded and supportive about raw feeding can be a great place to start! Or at least, one that does not harbour an obvious negative bias. You can find this out (sometimes) on the practice website, the vet's bio and by just simply asking your vet when you meet her.

2. Having a trusted relationship with your vet helps immensely in your credibility. So build that important relationship as soon as you can. The more she knows you, the more she will listen. (It works both ways, the more you know your vet, the more you will trust her!)

3. Providing scientific evidence like books and research papers may help. Vets are trained scientifically and many tend to base their decisions on proven knowledge. It gives them a better grounding for their choices.

4. Explaining your reasoning why you decided to try raw feeding can help her to sympathise. For example, if you had previous experiences that were successful or you simply believe it and/or interested in trying.

Remember that your vet is probably trying to give her best advice based on the knowledge she has. She cares deeply for you and your pet. It is nothing personal. You are your pet's guardian and you know (or will know!) what is best for your pet. Be confident and use your vet to achieve the best for you and your pet, regardless of what you feed.

Takeaway: There can be a few different reasons why your vet may not be receptive to 'non-conventional' veterinary medicine. It could be past experiences of her not getting expected results that she does not wish to repeat. It could be pure ignorance of the topic and hence not able to suggest, much less support it, as it would not be her best advice and irresponsible to do so. It is could be her personal beliefs. Regardless of all the reasons (and excuses), the true underlying reason is still to make sure that she is performing to the best of her ability and giving the best advice she can provide. It is really rare for a vet to not advise 'non-conventional' medicine out of spite.

ABSENCE OF PROOF IS NOT PROOF OF ABSENCE.

– William Cowper

So far, we have looked into a vet's mind and alternative veterinary medicine amongst many other topics. Let's now delve into one of the most common topics that causes disagreement between your vet and you... the cost of veterinary medicine.

MONEY, MONEY, MONEY –

IT'S A RICH VET'S WORLD...

OR IS IT?

Insights into the Value of Vet

Medicine

'You are a vet. You must be minted.' Many vets have heard that before. I know I have. 69% of pet guardians complain about vet fees (The Guardian, April 2016). Yet 54.5% of vet practices have a below average of profit margins of 8-12% (SPVS September 2016). Are vets charging too much? When should you discuss costs with your vet without feeling like you are being judged?

Here, we will discuss the cost of veterinary care, the reasons for it to be seemingly high and how that affects you, the pet guardian. More importantly, you will receive tips to improve understanding between your vet and you with your expectations and budgets. There will be a bonus section on how to save money at your vets.

- **You mean you have to pay?!**

The cost of veterinary medicine can be viewed in two ways. Firstly, it can be viewed as the cost to the business, i.e. the overheads, the equipment costs, the salaries paid, etc. Or it can be viewed as the cost to you, the pet guardian, i.e. how much you pay for your veterinary bills.

Cost to the business usually includes the site overheads (the rent, utility bills, building/practice insurance, permits, lawyer fees, maintenance of property, repairs, adhering to fire regulations, purchase/hire of equipment like washing machines, x-ray and general anaesthetic facilities. It also includes employment costs (salaries, pensions, registration fees, subscription fees, uniforms and personal equipment). Consumables and stock can play a definite cost as well (needles, syringes, suture materials, bandages, drugs, food and cleaning equipment). There are various other costs involved, some small and others large. The cost of running a veterinary practice can be quite substantial even for the simplest of set-ups. Usually, once surgical and hospitalisation facilities are involved, the cost will escalate quite considerably compared to a consulting/dispensing only model.

After the initial set-up costs are met, the running costs can also be hefty. For example, a building will require a fire alarm system and can spend thousands of pounds installing it and then a few hundred pounds annually to maintain it and as expected, in itself, it does not generate any income at all so it cannot really considered an investment in the strictest sense. The x-ray machine, autoclave steriliser and general anaesthetic machine have to be serviced yearly (some are legal requirements) regardless of whether it has been used once or a hundred times. To elaborate the background costs more, the canisters that hold the emergency oxygen are being rented on a daily basis and are unlikely to be used at all, but still need to be paid for. There are a lot of 'just-in-case' costs involved. For example, the cost of the x-ray facilities set-up including leaded walls/doors, x-ray generator and processors can cost tens of thousands and considering it may not be used regularly, it still exists and needs to be paid for. Considering more than 80% of interaction with you and treatment of your pet takes place in the consultation rooms and hardly ever leads to using the surgical, x-rays and hospitalisation facilities, it is incredible to think that the set-up for the latter is vastly more than the costs of the consulting rooms.

The cost to you, the pet guardian, is when the

veterinary facilities are being used whether it is consulting with the vet, receiving advice and/or treatment, further diagnostics and hospitalisation. Usually, it is incurred when your pet is sick and needing some form of advice and/or treatment. It is interesting to consider that veterinary medicine provides value in a not-ideal situation, like when your pet is sick or ill. Compared to many other business that provide a product or service that improves your current state, for example, a hairdresser provides value to improve your current hairdo to something better and you usually walk out feeling good about yourself as you have been 'improved'. Whereas at the vets (like dentists), you (or your pet) had to 'suffer', be a bit 'less' than what you (or your pet) were and the vet (or dentist) will provide value to regain the original form again. It is no wonder no one really likes going to the vets or the dentists! It almost implies something negative has happened when a visit is warranted. It is also not surprising for you to resent the cost of veterinary (or dental) treatment. Other businesses, we choose to frequent and pay for the products or services that we want to buy. If the price is too expensive, we can decline or choose to save before buying as it is of no rush and of no great consequence whether we have it immediately. However, at the vets, emotions can be highly charged as your pet is unwell and it is much harder to refuse a service and/or product as your pet remains needed treatment. Would you inform your dentist not to treat your painful tooth due to cost?

It is more of a 'reluctant' or 'no-choice' purchase because of a situation rather than a willing and joyous investment in a specifically desired outcome. You would never bring your happy, healthy pet into your vets and buy a veterinary service or product!

This section is not about moaning or lamenting about the high expense of running a vet practice. It is simply acknowledging the nature of veterinary services (and products) and reporting what it costs to run a vet practice.

- **What happens to every £100 charged?**

When you are presented with your vet bill, how do you feel? Do you perceive your vet must be 'doing very well' with what she is charging? After all, it can be considered quite a lot of money in some instances.

The amount of money you make is not as important as how much money is spent making that. For example, if it costs £1,000 to make £1,000, you are left with nothing in the end despite 'making' £1,000. This begs the question, "How profitable is veterinary services as a business?" or simply, what happens to every £100 charged?

Exact figures differ from practices but in general, the breakdown is as such. The government takes 20% (VAT). Staff cost usually accounts for 25% (+/- 3%). Stock like drugs, food, supplements and consumables like syringes, cleaning equipment usually takes 22 to 24%. Building rental, utility bills, computer system, diagnostic equipment (like x-rays, laboratory equipment), operating facilities (like the operating room, general anaesthetic equipment), specialised cleaning equipment (like autoclave, ultrasonic bath) and general license, insurance usually accounts for 22 to 24%, give or take. This leaves the profit for the business owner between 9-18%. This means that of every £100 charged, after paying all the necessary bills to generate that £100, about £9 to £18 is left for the business owner, making the profit margin 9-18%. Even if the business owner gave up all profits, it would only amount to less than 20% discount, still leaving a sizable bill to be paid. Not many people would regard that as a great business.

By extension, if your veterinary consultation is £40, it would mean that you are paying your vet between £3.60-£7.20 (9-18%) for her five-year university education (plus working years' experience). That is the cost of a coffee and muffin at Costas for professional medical advice. Would you consider that to be of great value?

Having a chat with one of my best clients who own a fish and chip van, I asked, "Sophie, may I ask what your profit margin is?"

She replied, "50%."

I was astounded. In veterinary practice, I have learnt from my previous bosses and the general business courses that the industry aims for the much coveted 20% profit margin and not many practices are achieving anywhere close to that at all.

I was curious and pressed on. "May I know what your turnover was last year?"

"£80,000," she replied.

"Does that mean that you took home (as profit) £40,000?" I queried.

"Yes," she replied.

I considered that deeply. If I were to apply the vet business model and achieved the coveted 20% profit margin, to have a profit of £40,000, the vet practice would have to make £200,000 a year. Except as it is over the VAT allowance of £83,000 a year, the practice would have to make £250,000 a year to include the VAT.

So, if your child was to ask you, "I would like to earn £40,000, what should I do?"

Your reply may be something like, "You can study five years to be a vet, start a business and make £250,000 a year or own a fish and chip van and make £80,000 a year to earn £40,000." It simply means that, compared to highly profitable businesses, vets have to charge more to make the same amount of money.

(For my own curiosity, I checked what the profit margin was for the burger van not far from my practice. It was 42%. N.B. Both businesses have had their vehicles and

equipment fully paid off.)

Just before I am accused for being money-minded, the point is that there are a lot of more profitable businesses compared to veterinary medicine. It may be expensive to receive veterinary treatment but it just is the cost of medical services, not because your vet is making a huge profit.

The purpose of this information is not to gather sympathy but simply to state the fact that 1. Your vet is NOT in for the money (as this is NOT a good way to make money) and 2. Your vet does NOT make that much money (much contrary to popular belief!). She (and vet nurses) chose this profession because of her profound respect and love for the animals. In addition, she has a sincere desire to help you and other pet guardians. If it was about the money, she would have chosen something else. A business with much higher profit margins and not so many overheads!

I hope this has exposed a fallacy that simply is not true that the veterinary profession makes easy money. If your vet does well, she has worked extremely hard for it is certainly not easy money!

- **Vets must be paid a lot!**

Vets are considered to be professionals like doctors, dentists, lawyers and accountants. You would think the salaries would be similar, right?

Check this out...

➤ A trainee lawyer (for about two years) in the UK earns an average of £37,000 (ranging from £27,000 to £50,000). Once fully qualified, it increases to an average of £62,000 (ranging from £42,000 to £90,000). American firms can pay up to £143,000. An equity partner earns an average of £130,000.

➤ A newly qualified accountant earns between £38,000 to £47,000 yearly. With experience, it increases to an average of £62,000 (ranging from £11,000 to £400,000).

➤ In the NHS, a newly qualified doctor earns between £28,200 to £32,700 yearly. During consultant training (about seven years), it rises to £38,700 to £49,000. As a consultant, it ranges from £79,000 to £107,000 increasing with experience.

➤ A newly qualified dentist in the NHS earns £32,800. An experienced NHS dentist earns an average of £63,665 (up to £98,000). Like the doctors, a dentist consultant's salary ranges between £80,000 and £107,000.

What about vets? More specifically, vets in practice (as compared to working in a corporate drug company) like your vet. So, a typical package for a newly qualified vet is £33,500. Most companion animal vets earn about £46,400 a year. If they obtained further qualifications, it may sometimes (not guaranteed) increase to £50,000 - £65,000. These salaries remain very similar for the rest of their career.

- **The Amazing Free Health Care (National Health Services, UK)**

Due to the awesome existence of the National Health Services (NHS), the majority of UK residents do not possess a poor concept of medical costs or value, instead they possess NO concept of them. Please do not misunderstand, I have nothing against the NHS. In fact, I love the NHS as it has provided much help and assurance in the times when my family and I needed it. It certainly provides peace of mind knowing that our medical needs are covered. However, as it exists in its present state, the UK public does not understand how much it costs to provide a medical service. No prices or costs are usually discussed. There has been abuse of usage.

It is all paid using tax payers' money. For example, you may moan when your vet's consultation is £50, especially if only advice had been sought and no treatment was needed. Are you aware that it costs £150 when you see your GP for an NHS appointment? Sometimes the consultation may be short, no medication is prescribed and all you receive is peace of mind that still costs £150. In veterinary medicine, there are times where no treatment is needed and only advice is given but the perception of not receiving physical treatment whether in form of injections or tablets, no value may be perceived and some pet guardians (not all!) may question the fee charged as 'nothing was done at all'.

Another perfect example would be hip replacements. A hip replacement for a dog or cat may range between £4,500-£6,000 usually depending on size and surgeon. That may seem like a hefty sum to you but did you know that it costs the NHS £12,000 for a hip replacement in a human? Hip replacements are considered to be a fairly standard procedure, with approximately 130,000 being done each year and the number is rising. Arguably, hip replacements in dogs and cats would be considered more difficult as not only are the bones smaller and more delicate (easier to break), a larger range of implants have to be stocked for the size differences. Also, vets do not have the luxury of the economies of scale (the cost per implant may be more as a smaller number compared to how human implants are manufactured). All these factors should make the cost of hip replacement in pets much higher or at least similar to those in humans but instead it is about half the price. This is despite using similar anaesthetic equipment, similar training and similar implants. Isn't that interesting?

It is not anyone's fault for this ignorance. A suggestion would be for the NHS to provide the patients and their families using their service with the invoice. I am not saying they have to pay but it would allow them to appreciate what the treatment had cost. Not only will they be more educated and aware of what medical care costs, it may even allow more appreciation for this marvellous health system and we certainly would not take it for granted.

- **Vets know about animals, not business**

Vets are not natural businessmen. They are simply not trained like that. Asking a vet about business is like getting a baking recipe from a cobbler. As such, prices are generally determined by the neighbouring practices, the competitors. Most vets are just interested in treating the animals which is why many became vets in the first place. Building a good profitable business can be extremely daunting for anyone, much more if you have no clue, like a vet. As discussed, due to the NHS, vets also have not much to look up or refer to in terms of charging for medical value. The typical vet is pretty academic, usually extremely competent in treating animals, some may be good communicators but very few are good businessmen.

It is made even harder as the profession also struggles with their value. Remember that the veterinary profession is served by the NHS which also means that it is likely that they have no idea what their value is and merely base their prices on what their neighbouring vet practices charge.

This has led to the relatively low fees (compared to medical fees in health care) and with the comparatively high overheads, it is not surprising that the profit margin can be very small.

• **Pet insurance? Don't need it!**

In Sweden, 90% of dogs are insured. In UK, only 25% of dogs and 12% of cats are insured. This is very interesting as the UK public has an extremely sympathetic view towards animals. Animal welfare is fairly important in this country and there are plenty of charity and rescue pets available. However, when it comes to insuring your pet so medical costs need not be an issue, comparatively, it is not very well received at all. Isn't that interesting?

This could be due to a few reasons, where pet guardians are willing to spend a good amount of money purchasing the animals (some spend thousands on buying a pet, pedigree or not!) but do not invest in pet insurance. Firstly, the provision of the NHS has obscured the cost of medical treatment so they are simply not aware of how expensive medical treatment can be. Secondly, the NHS may give a sense of false assurance that medical services are free or cheap as no one pays the NHS directly. Thirdly, the cost of veterinary fees in

UK is actually not very high comparatively so people do not see the point of getting their pets insured. For example, the cost for a vet consultation in Sweden is usually 150€ (about £125) compared to the UK price of about £25 (in little towns) to £60-70 (in larger cities). Fourthly, it is the lack of awareness of animals falling sick. Many people just (for no good reason) presume their pet will not fall sick! Lastly, it could be historical that their previous pets were never insured and hence they do not see the point. Or they had the last pet insured but did not make any claims and thus, perceived a waste of money, of no value and unnecessary. Pet guardians who have claimed on their insurance in the past tend to be the ones that will get their pets insured, whereas others who have not, tend not to see the point.

Either way, the proportion of insured pets in the UK is very low compared to some European countries. This is a very particular situation considering the UK is well-known as a nation of 'animal lovers', yet the uptake of a valid and effective method of covering medical costs (pet insurance) is so low.

Is your pet insured? If not, what are your reasons for holding back?

- **When is best to discuss cost with your vet**

A simple analogy I would use would be: 'When would

you discuss your personal beliefs (like if you are wanting to start a family, your religion or your dietary preference) with your partner?' I believe the answer to that would be AS SOON AS POSSIBLE.

Many pet guardians (and many vets as well!) do not like to talk about finances and expectation of costs in general, as though it makes them seemingly 'money grabbing' or 'care more about money' than the pet. Is that really true? Is it not your responsibility as your pet's guardian to make sure that you can actually afford your pet's care including possible medical bills? So many pet guardians have this illogical notion that their pets will never fall ill.

It is not only some pet guardians that have this aversion. The vet profession suffers from it too. From the front desk, to the nursing team and finally the vets, the interest in discussing finance is never a priority. In fact, in my experience, the best group of people that seemed more likely to be able to discuss finance, is the front of house compared to the medical team. Most of the profession like to focus on treating the animal and making sure they get better seemingly with little or no concern to finance. The level of confidence displayed when discussing medical treatment far outshines and excels that displayed when discussing how much that medical treatment would cost.

It is almost cultural for you and your vet to shun the topic of cost except to say that it can be 'very high' and 'expensive'. Somehow, the topic of cost has been made taboo to all, as though if money was discussed, the care for your pet is less. It is just simply not true. Money should be discussed because that is a reality. Just like you would find out the price of anything you buy, it should be the same with your pet. Pets cost money when they fall ill. Vet medicine costs money to help ill pets.

What if it was different? What if there was another way? What if, all parties could approach the topic of cost as outright and frank as possible from the start, like how you would tell your spouse whether you want children or not from the beginning? Would that not bring extreme clarity to all on how to proceed? It is not a topic to be shunned. It is a responsibility to be met to reduce any difficult conversations regarding finance in future. We should be discussing it with the same amount of energy as any other aspect of your pet's life like choice of food, vaccination, training, etc.

The idea of cost does not go away just because we do not discuss it. If your vet knows your financial expectations, it allows her to provide a more tailored approach for you. Not better or worse, just more suitable. If the expectations are known, respected and agreed upon from the beginning, there should not be any awkwardness but only the best approach to be presented for the good of your pet and you.

• Moving forward

Finances (or lack of) can cause massive headaches for you when your pet is unwell. The feeling of guilt, helplessness and sometimes rage can affect you greatly. It really can have profound effects on your mood, feelings, day and life. It robs your joy, peace and the purpose of having a pet.

Perhaps a suggestion would be to not put yourself in that position in the first place. This usually requires a mind-set shift. It would be to presume that your pet may fall ill (because he may, to different degrees!) and when he does, it may cost money to get him better again. It may seem like an obvious idea to you but there are many that do not believe that. They believe that (for some unknown reason) their pet will always stay healthy. It could be perhaps because of past experiences where their pets have remained relatively healthy and not needed any medical intervention. So, by extension, their current pets are expected to be the same. It just simply is not true. They live in hope. Are you able to relate?

When you have accepted that your pet may need medical care at some point in time, the only question that remains is how you will afford it. There are two obvious choices. The first one is for you to pay. As your pet's guardian, you have the responsibility to your pet for providing medical care as much as providing food and shelter for them. The second option that may be available in some countries is pet insurance. Pet insurance does not buy health but it buys peace of mind that when something happens, you need not use cost as a deciding factor for which treatment option to choose.

An important conversation to be had with your vet would be regarding finances. Whether you have invested in pet insurance or not, it is always beneficial for both of you to establish mutual expectations. This would allow better understanding leading to increased trust and respect for your vet and you. You will feel better as your vet knows your expectations and you have less fear of what she may think when you make decisions. Your vet will feel more confident in treating your pet as she knows what you want. It will reduce stress by an enormous amount for your vet and you, enabling the most suitable and appropriate treatment for your pet.

The issue usually lies when the cost is unexpected, coupled with the stress as your pet is unwell. The problem is that it is not easy to know the cost of medical treatments until you need them. It is abnormal to research the cost of diseases (unless it is breed related possibly or due to past experiences) unless it happens to your pet. It may be wiser to expect it and make sure there are sufficient funds (whether by insurance or personal) to cover any issues should it happen, than to live in fear hoping that nothing will go wrong.

It is really important to be able to communicate freely

with your vet.

Another suggestion would be for you to consider your pet as a luxury, not an entitlement. If you are not able to afford to take care of his every need, in health and sickness, perhaps you have to ask yourself if you should have a pet at all. You may be better off without the stress and angst and your pet may be better off where his needs can be met. I sincerely apologise if I offend you by saying this. My intention is not to offend but to keep us accountable and aware that having a pet is a huge responsibility. It comes from a place of deep care where I wish you are never found in a situation where you feel stress and guilt for the inability to provide for your pet. Pet guardianship should be enjoyable (including all the challenges that come with it!) and not seen as an undesirable burden.

Takeaway: The cost of vet bills can often be very (seemingly) high due to various reasons including steep operating costs and the lack of information regarding medical value due to poor education from the veterinary profession and the NHS. It is important to be able to frankly discuss your cost expectations with your vet. No price is too high for success and any price is too high for failure. A suggestion would be to focus on value instead of a numerical cost. Your pet can fall ill and the price to get him back to health again is often not factored in. The best tip I can offer is to chat with your vet, be honest about your expectations, learn more about the profession from your trusted vet and don't be afraid to talk about money.

WHAT YOU PAY IS THE COST.

WHAT YOU RECEIVE IS THE VALUE.

After learning about the cost of veterinary medicine and how best to avoid discontentment with your vet, we will be exploring crossing the rainbow bridge, when your pet transits from the human world to pet heaven... euthanasia.

WE ALL DIE

Euthanasia:

A Discussion

Life is a terminal affair. This is a singular event that binds all living creatures together; the fact that our lives must end eventually. Your vet belongs to the only profession in the world that discusses euthanasia on a fairly regular basis. Your pet's life is more likely to be ended by euthanasia than passing away naturally. Do you feel euthanasia always marks an end or a beginning?

Here, you will learn more about euthanasia, some considerations regarding the decisions made for it and quality of life. You will also find out more about how it is performed and how it works. You will also learn how euthanasia impacts pet guardians and vets. Last but not least, you will discover how euthanasia does not mean the end for some.

- ## Time to say Goodbye

Euthanasia means 'good death' in Greek. It is an act that your vet may perform to end your pet's life, usually by a lethal injection. The reasons for euthanasia can vary from compromised quality of life to practical reasons like overcrowding in some rescue centres.

You would think there must be in-depth advanced training to handle such an important and delicate procedure! It is not exactly true.

Very simply, there was no formal training in Vet College that teaches your vet how to discuss euthanasia. She was trained to perform euthanasia with the safest, least stressful and most effective method. However, she may not have training in discussing the topic of euthanasia, the short- and long-term implications of this process with you. Usually, it relies more on your vet's personality, her past experiences and the situation itself where the most appropriate interaction is presented.

As such, what you feel may range from being greatly traumatised as no emotional support was offered to a completely positive, life-changing experience as all your emotion needs were met to say goodbye to your pet.

Considering this is potentially a transformative event, the process of euthanasia should be much more than just putting your pet to sleep as effectively and stress-free as possible. It should include more support for you before, during and after the procedure as well.

• I don't want to see my pet suffer

In my first job, I had to euthanise a 17-year-old cat with kidney failure. The guardians had been caring for him for 18 months since it was diagnosed. They made sure the food was wet and fluids were always provided, keeping him hydrated. They invested in diets that were kinder to the failing kidneys. They provided supplements to support the insufficiencies of those important bean-shaped organs. They did all they could to make their pet as comfortable as possible. In the end, they monitored his quality of life very carefully and when it was compromised, they requested the needle of no return.

Discussing quality of life is something that your vet does on a fairly regular basis. There are multiple situations when this topic is brought up. Some examples include after the diagnosis of a terminal condition (like cancer, organ failure), when an animal is slowly but surely showing signs of being affected by a chronic condition (like osteoarthritis, failing sight), after a traumatic incident that has affected multiple organs or just simply caused vast amounts of damage that will require intensive medical care and recovery. Usually, these conversations are held if euthanasia is a possible option.

These discussions are all different to each situation as each circumstance is unique. There are no set parameters that are measured or philosophies that are imposed simply because your pet has a unique lifestyle and you have a unique set of beliefs.

171

For example, Bear was an absolutely adorable, lively two-year-old Labrador that suffered a spinal injury which resulted in him being doubly incontinent (he leaked urine and faeces as he could not hold them in). He belonged to a young childless couple who absolutely doted on him. Apart from his double incontinence, he was as right as rain, running and jumping like any other dog would do. You wouldn't know the difference! So, for four years, his guardians used nappies and changed them religiously two to three times daily. Their commitment meant that not only their beloved dog was kept clean; their house was not subjected to soiling too. It was only when he unfortunately contracted cancer, did they make the hard decision to put him to sleep. This may seemed like a fairly extreme case (to apply multiple nappies daily for years) but it is true. Now, this arrangement may be suitable for these guardians but could you imagine if the same dog (with the same issues) belonging to a family having young children, toddlers or babies? It probably would have resulted in a different outcome for Bear.

Simba was an indoor blind cat that had no interest in roaming the streets like his feline counterparts. So having no vision was of no consequence to him as he had memorised the layout of the entire house and also relied on his other senses to compensate for his lack of sight. However, the considerations would be different if Simba loved going out in the midst of traffic, roads, and the neighbourhood's bushes, and would be miserable if kept indoors.

Every discussion about the quality of life for your pet is different. Your vet has to consider the temperament of your pet (what he likes to do, what his habits are), the exact consequences of the present condition (how it is going to affect your pet) and you (your beliefs, lifestyle, expectations and how well you can cope/adjust to the situation). There are never set rules on this wide discussion and there never should be. In these potentially emotionally charged situations, your vet, as a professional, needs to help you to understand the thoughts behind quality of life. It starts with actually finding out more about your expectations and beliefs before even giving any advice.

Only by understanding what you are thinking of, can your vet give the most suitable advice. If done properly with compassion and without compromise on your pet's welfare, she is more likely to achieve a result that will not entail guilt, confusion, but actually encompasses understanding and the feeling that you are doing the right thing and everyone (including your pet) will benefit from the outcome. It is not easy and usually when there is a negative outcome for anyone involved (your pet, you or your vet), it is usually due to some form of communication breakdown and misunderstanding.

• I have had enough

In the previous chapter, we discussed the quality of life of pets and using that information to decide when is the appropriate time for euthanasia. Here, we will discuss your quality of life, your pet's guardian, the wonderful pet carer. There is a term, 'caring for the carer', coined by Andrew Hale (Dog Behaviourist) which is extremely relevant in this context.

It would be fair to say that you are good at gauging the quality of life of your pet(s) and making the right decision at the right time. You are a great carer for your pet(s). However, who is caring for you, the carer?

In the bond between your pet and you, there lies not one but two parties involved. The quality of life of you (and your family), the pet guardian, is just as important as your pet's. You must not forget to take care of yourself.

Munchkin is an eight-year-old cat that suffered from kidney failure belonging to a family with two toddlers. Despite extensive treatment to manage his failed kidneys, he was urinating whenever it suited him on multiple occasions in the house. The smell was overpowering and hugely unpleasant. His guardians, a young couple, struggled for months, trying to keep their house clean and odour-free. It was a massive health hazard and detrimental for their toddlers. They felt helplessness and despair at the same time. It was only when they made the decision to rehome Munchkin to someone who was more equipped to take care of his special needs, did they manage to remain sane and retain hygiene which was desperately needed. They felt relieved and guilty at the same time. It took months before they finally accepted that they had made the right choice. They realised that their quality of life was suffering when they were caring for Munchkin. They simply did not realise that until later. Can you imagine the guilt in giving up your pet and also the relief in doing so?

A four-year-old Husky named Congo had attacked his guardian's daughter. He had been a slightly nervous dog since being rescued when he was two years old. He would react violently to any sound or visual triggers, especially to the sound of the recycling truck and seeing bearded men. His guardian had always been able to manage him without issue and he had never attempted to show aggression towards him. However, one day, Congo attacked and bit his guardian's daughter for no apparent reason. His daughter received 12 stitches at the local hospital, became fearful of Congo and no longer enjoyed his company. This incident really affected the trust between Congo and his guardian. At last, a very difficult decision was made to have him euthanised due to the mistrust and the inability to rehome him. It was an extremely traumatising time for his guardian and his quality of life suffered before and after making the painful decision. Have you found yourself in a similar situation before? How did you manage it?

Discussing your pet's and/or your quality of life can be tremendously challenging. It is equally contentious to determine whose quality of life is more important, your pet's or yours. On one hand, you may say that you chose to have your pet to improve your quality of life and thus, you come first in consideration and if your quality of life is compromised, you make decisions to improve your situation. On the other hand, you may feel that you have a responsibility to your pet that you have elected to care for and regardless of situation, you have to do everything in your power to ensure that his quality of life is preserved even if it means that yours may be compromised as a result. So, where do you stand and is the other view necessarily of lesser importance?

You may have bent over backwards, compromised your happiness, starved as you have spent all your money on your pets and even suffered from anxiety, stress and depression trying to maintain your pet's quality of life. When is it too much? Where do you draw the line that says that enough is enough? Do you even draw the line at all?

You have a responsibility to yourself (and your human family) first and foremost. If you are not able to take care of yourself, you are doing your (human) family a disservice. Also, when you are not well, ether physically or mentally, your pets that you love will pick that up as well and be affected. You need to care for the carer, you. You must not forget about yourself. It can be very easy to get carried away, to care for another and neglect yourself in the process. Remember to be kind to yourself.

- **This is ridiculously difficult, too painful and impossible to bear**

Bringing your pet to your vet and leaving without him is never an easy thing. The feelings that follow after giving consent for euthanasia can be overpowering and vastly different for different people. You may feel relief (immensely at times), profound sadness, despair, guilt, fear, anger, resentment, self-reproach, gratitude and/or emptiness. These feelings could be short or long term. Over time, they may change as well as you digest and work your feelings from one to another. The impact on you can be quite profound. You may recover fast or you may never recover. They are all valid, normal and personal feelings that you need to acknowledge, understand and embrace.

Iris, a caring and sensitive pet guardian, went to her vet six months after her ferret had been put to sleep. She was still wracked with guilt over whether she made the right choice to euthanise him. There was no doubt in her vet's mind that it was the right thing to do as he was suffering despite all treatment and she had clearly made the right call. However, Iris had not been able to reconcile with herself. It took some time to allow her to come to terms and she finally could let it go.

How you process events is exclusive and different from others. The important thing is that you process it and not ignore the feelings. Your vet may have played an important role in you and your pet's life. It may be sensible to engage in a conversation with her regarding your feelings. Sometimes it can be difficult as it is not usually done (or if she had assisted in the euthanasia itself). Sometimes, that may bring a sense of peace and resolution. Repressed feelings lead to pain eventually. Find the strength in you. You know it is there.

- **Euthanasia – the Specifics and Technique**

In most cases, euthanasia of your pet, dog or cat, is performed by giving an overdose of an injectable anaesthetic drug. As it suggests, your pet will fall asleep as though he is going under general anaesthesia except that it is an overdose and he does not wake up.

A sedation can be given (you can request for a sedation from your vet if you want) so your pet becomes sleepier and not as aware of his surroundings before injecting the overdose of anaesthetic. The sedation drug is usually injected into your pet's muscle. The final injection is usually given into a vein (most commonly used is the front leg cephalic vein) but your vet may choose to inject into other suitable areas if considered appropriate, for example, the kidney.

Once the anaesthetic has been given, your pet's heart and breathing rates slow down and eventually stop completely. This process can take seconds to minutes. Your vet will usually check the heart to make sure it is no longer beating. She may also check the eye (corneal) reflex by gently tapping the eyeball. There should be no response.

When your pet has passed away, the muscle holding the urine (bladder sphincter) and faeces (anus) may relax and he may urinate or defecate. Also, his breathing reflex may kick in despite the lack of heart beat or eye reflex and he may take several deep breaths continuously. This only happens in a small group of animals. Please do not be alarmed as it is purely a reflex and happens after death has occurred. Your vet may warn you of both events.

In extremely rare occasions (usually in very sick or dehydrated pets), where a vein may not be obtained, your vet may give the injection into the belly or the heart. Please do let your vet know if you are uncomfortable with that.

Euthanasia for other species may differ so it is important to find out more about it from your vet.

- ## The Non-Monetary Price of Performing Euthanasia

Advances in animal care industry in the past three decades have coincided with growing integration of companion animals in people's families. How you view your pet is vastly different from how you may have 30 years ago. In Australia, the pet population is greater than the human population. In the USA, more people live with a pet than a child. The role of your vet has been extended from short-term pain and acute medical care of your pet to include your long-term emotional well-being. This can get complicated when end-of-life decisions need to be made. Though the idea of euthanasia is a good death, the choice to first convey it and next to rationalise it during decision-making can be complicated. It can trigger feelings of guilt and negative emotions for you and your vet.

Your vet is five times more likely to be present when your pet dies than your doctor will be for you. Your pet may present at the brink of death requiring euthanasia through trauma, illness, injury, possible abuse and even abandonment. In addition, your pet may be presented because you are not able to consent to medical procedures sometimes due to cost or personal circumstances. This can trigger strong feelings of conflict and psychological distress for your vet. She may be forced to behave in ways that conflict with her personal beliefs. She may find herself in moral distress when waiting for you to make a decision, prolonging your pet's suffering. She may also find it a stressful challenge caring for your pet while simultaneously managing your emotional distress.

The euthanasia process is so much more complicated than just the act of euthanasia itself. When the procedure is completed, your vet may then have to provide support for you when you are grieving. You may discover when coping with ongoing grieving issues, your friends and family may set a time limit on how appropriate it is to mourn for your pet. This means that you may turn to your vet as a source of comfort and support. Your vet is not likely to be trained as a grief counsellor and she may grapple with your emotions.

The emotional pressures associated with the entire euthanasia process may thus undermine your vet's wellbeing. The value of your vet carrying all these burdens cannot be underestimated.

There is no price that can be placed on her providing such value to you. Please do take care of your vet. There is no other job that entails such trauma, responsibility and stress to a point where it is evident that job dissatisfaction, high turnover, relationship issues, physical and mental health issues and elevated suicide rate is present.

- **Your Pet's Euthanasia Plan**

This extremely important topic has been neglected and avoided for (good) reasons. You probably do not like to talk about death unless absolutely needed, especially when your pet is healthy. However, I urge you to think differently.

Discussing euthanasia at the puppy vaccinations or in an extremely young dog (though some pet guardians differ and have discussed that with me in the past when their pet was very young) may be excessive. However, discussing it at some point in time especially when your pet is getting older may not only be reasonable but also wise.

The advantages for doing so include:

1. Aligning your vet to your views regarding euthanasia

2. Allowing your vet to know your wishes when the time comes. For example, whether you would prefer a home visit, cremation (with or without ashes returned) or home burial

3. Allowing your vet to understand your views and measures regarding quality of life

4. The choice to pay for the euthanasia in advance if you prefer.

Discussions of the above topics before a potentially stressful situation will allow you to make clear decisions with a lucid, unstressed mind.

• **It's not all Doom and Gloom**

You may actually feel liberated after your pet has crossed the rainbow bridge. You may certainly feel sad. However, you are now able to make choices that you could not make before. It opens a whole world of possibilities. You may have felt physically tied down by your pet in the past and now you can actually go travelling without feeling guilty for getting someone else to take care of your pet. You may make use of the space that your pet used to occupy and convert it to something else. You may change your lifestyle, going to places that you could not previously go to because of your pet. You may even embark on a new career that you could not before with the commitment of your pet. So for you, the end may just be the beginning.

IT IS NOT THE YEARS IN THE LIFE THAT COUNTS,

BUT THE LIFE IN THE YEARS.

Takeaway: How you view euthanasia can differ greatly depending on your beliefs, culture, past experiences and personal opinions. No one opinion is more 'right' or better than another. The decision on when and how euthanasia should be performed usually depends on the assessment of your pet's quality of life and that can differ greatly too. Everyone grieves differently after the euthanasia. You may have better coping mechanisms in place than others. You may grieve 'successfully' while others may not. Your pet's euthanasia may mark auspicious beginnings for your future. There are advantages to discussing euthanasia with your vet before it is needed.

You have learnt a great deal about various views of vets and pet guardians, from veterinary medicine to pet guardianship, from how your vet is trained (or not) in complementary medicine and finally from the cost of veterinary medicine to euthanasia. In the last chapter, you will find out why it is beneficial to have a successful relationship with your vet.

THEE, ME, WE

(WE ARE ON THE SAME TEAM!)

Working Together So Our Pet

Wins

'Caring for animals isn't what I do, it is what I am.' That is something you may say. Let me let you in on a secret... Your vet probably thinks the same way too! The reality is that both your vet and you provide care for your pet, just in different ways.

In this last chapter, you will understand the need for a successful relationship between your vet and you. You will learn the steps of building a great alliance with your vet. You will see the benefits of a winning partnership between your vet and you. You will also discover the ultimate winner from this cooperation.

• Let's just be friends

The idea of having a relationship with your vet may seem alien to some. After all, you are used to NOT seeing your vet unless there are issues. Seeing your vet usually has negative associations like your pet being ill, high expenses and is fraught with plenty of unknowns (causing stress). It is almost like seeing your dentist, you never really want to do so unless absolutely necessary.

However, if you treat your pet like your family member, you may find it beneficial to have a trusted vet, one to whom you can voice your worries and concerns regarding his care. In moments of need, you find it reassuring knowing that your vet who understands you (and shares the same beliefs and expectations) would be the one giving medical advice. The bond between your pet and you has dramatically increased in recent times and the amount of relief may be considerable going to your trusted vet compared to a complete stranger.

If your pet has a long and/or complicated medical past, it is certainly easier and more effective seeing your vet that knows his medical history intimately to save time and cost.

If you suffer from stress, seeing a trusted familiar face would certainly reduce the stress involved.

If your personal expectations and beliefs have been addressed, understood and respected beforehand, it makes medical treatment discussion smoother and more appropriate, especially regarding quality of life and financial costs.

When effort is made to build a meaningful relationship with your vet, the benefits are in abundance. For you to know that you have a trusted ally that is integral to your pet's health is extremely valuable. The satisfaction and security derived from such an alliance has been described as 'priceless' and 'reassuring' by pet guardians and vets alike. It is almost like having your own personal doctor for your pet. For your vet, the sense of fulfilment derived from helping not only your pet but also you can lead to greater job satisfaction and bring about a greater sense of purpose of making a true difference in her life. For your pet, the benefits are most obvious as the swiftest and tailor-made care can be provided that aligns to his guardian and his doctor.

- **What makes a Great Vet?**

Excellent question, it depends on who you ask!

If you ask your vet, she would probably say that extensive knowledge and the ability to treat the pet and get it better (clinical resolution) would be considered desirable traits. She may extend this to include good communication skills and being able to express empathy.

If you ask other pet guardians, many (not all!) would rate how they perceive the vet to care for their pet, understanding their (the guardian's, not the pet's) personal situation and possessing 'heart' above clinical knowledge. Some have said, "I don't care how much you know as long as I know that you care."

Other desirable traits include being a good listener, humble, easily accessible, the ability to speak in simple terms and possessing patience.

You will want and expect different things (compared to others) from your vet. It is almost like asking, "What makes a great partner?" It depends on what you are looking for. It is similar in choosing your vet. The more important question to ask is, "As a pet guardian, what sort of vet am I wanting to fit my needs and expectations?" then start looking for the vet that best fits you. Your idea of a great vet may differ a lot to others. It is not right or wrong, better or worse. It is just different.

So, what do you want in a vet? Is it someone who is extremely knowledgeable? Or someone who understands your pet and you? Or simply someone who cares? If you are like many pet guardians I know, you will want everything!

Remember, your vet, your choice.

• What makes a Great Pet Guardian?

That is another excellent question.

Many pet guardians (like vets!) like to think that they are great pet guardians. And they may not be wrong! It depends on what the idea of 'great' is. You may provide the basic needs so your pet is free from diseases, malnutrition, discomfort, fear and is able to express normal behaviour (the Five Freedoms). That may be considered 'great'.

Or you may be much more involved and feel solely providing the basic needs is not enough. Speaking from a personal and professional point of view, pet guardians who actively maintain their pet's health, understand their needs, pay attention to their normal behaviour, are genuinely interested in them and understand the financial responsibility seem to gain more from their relationship with their pet. They are also much easier and more fulfilling to work with. It makes your vet's job much more straightforward as she can gather more information, build a great rapport and is able to do what is in the best interests for your pet without compromise due to cost or your disinterest. It allows her to express her skills much more effectively when treating your pet.

I urge you to get involved as much as you can in your pet's life if you want to get the most out of your relationship with him. 'How much you put in is how much you get out' certainly rings true in this instance.

If you feel your relationship with your pet is quite superficial and you want to get more out of it, you are in luck! Because you can do it! Properly study your pet, spend more (quality) time with him and understand his behaviour as much as you can. You will be rewarded in ways that you cannot imagine. It is like exploring a new relationship, how far and how deep you can stretch it only depends on your imagination and the effort you put into it.

If you have embraced the entirety of pet guardianship and love every second of it, congratulations! You know exactly what I mean and I commend you in allowing yourself to fully immerse into your fabulous pet. The bond between your pet and you is not only unique and special, it is also your personal achievement.

- **How to Form an Awesome and Stunning Pet Guardian-Vet relationship...**

First and foremost, you have to want it. It is so much simpler (and easier) having a transactional relationship, not unlike paying for your groceries at the checkout counter or shopping online. You have a need (your pet that needs treating) and your vet does just that. There is simply no further need for anything more. If your want is simply fulfilling a need and there is no desire to improve your relationship with your vet, you can stop reading now.

However, I know that you are not superficial and want more as you are reading this book! If you desire a transformational (not purely transactional) relationship, where all parties (your pet, your vet and you) emerge improved and actually benefit not only physically but also emotionally and spiritually, here are some steps that will help you achieve your goals.

Step 1. Speak Up!

Behind any powerfully effective relationship, powerfully effective communication is involved. Mind reading is still a sacred art left to mind readers, and neither you nor your vet is one. Without the power of mind reading, we have to articulate our thoughts and desires via mortal ways, usually by talking or sometimes in writing. Effective communication can be defined as *message sent, message received and message acted upon.* Any missing part in this three-step process usually results in communication breakdown.

It has been said that face-to-face communication is only 7% verbal, 38% tonal (non-verbal) and 55% body language (non-verbal). With this astounding finding, it is no wonder that it is not really what you say but HOW you say it using tonality and body language that affects the result of your message being passed on correctly, creating your desired outcome.

Not many people are trained to communicate effectively. In addition, the widespread availability of technology these days actually reduces the need for face-to-face communication thus further alienating skills in effective communication.

Your vet, in all likelihood will not be specifically trained in communication. Only in recent years has communication studies been part of the vet curriculum and it may not be enough. Your vet would be extremely well versed in the knowledge of diagnosing and treating multiple conditions but not very good at diagnosing and treating your concerns and worries. Even with the best intentions in mind, it is not unusual for your vet to treat your pet's presenting problem and think that it addresses all your concerns when that is only the superficial problem. An example would be purely treating your cat with itchy skin, resolving (or successfully managing) the issue but not understanding or addressing your worries that the issue might have caused for you. Sometimes, just acknowledging your worries and reassuring you that it is not your fault that your cat is itchy goes a long way. It brings more goodwill to all, including the vet profession.

Step 2. Don't Give Up!

You may have heard that 'patience is a virtue'. In this case, it is more that 'persistence is required!' Your vet may not be aware (unlike you) of the need to create an awesome relationship. After all, it was not emphasised in Vet College! You may need to be patient with her. There is a higher chance that she will understand the advantages of forming this unique bond with you over time, but not instantly.

Understand that the idea of building a powerful relationship with you, your pet's amazing guardian, may be as alien to your vet as it is to other pet guardians (not you, as you are reading this book!). So empathy, or more specifically, the lack of empathy in this case, may be present and you should not let that deter you from creating your formidable relationship with her. She may just need more time (don't we all?). You can be the one to show her!

Once both your vet and you are on board on this amazing journey, patience and empathy are still needed. Like any relationship, it does take time to foster a great one, much less an awesome and stunning one. Keep working at it. Improve and increase your communication. Remember that your vet's interaction and understanding of you and your pet is limited to the consultation room only for that set period of time, usually 15 minutes or less. This means that your vet really does not know too much about you at all (even if she wants to!) simply because of the lack of time and opportunity. It really does NOT mean that she is not interested. She just simply can't. So to allow greater understanding (even if it is a tiny bit which is more than nothing), remember that every little bit of communication helps. Written notes left or emails sent regarding your pet and you are important. It goes a very long way in improving your vet's understanding and appreciation of your life outside the consultation room.

When your vet knows more about you and your pet (beyond a consultation room), not only can the start of a wonderful relationship start, better and more appropriate treatment recommendations can be offered.

Step 3. Knowing Me Knowing You

Once a mutual understanding is achieved, that is when trust can be built. It could merely be an initial mutual understanding that improves over time. Only when the seed is planted, can you nurture it. It is impossible to improve something that is not there. When your vet understands your goals, beliefs and expectations of what you want from your pet or the bond with your pet, she will be more empowered to give you the most suitable (arguably defined as 'best') treatment options for your pet and you. Your vet wants to provide the best treatment for your pet except she does not know how without understanding your goals, beliefs and expectations. So, you are actually helping your vet a great deal by providing that information to her! She may even thank you for it!

In addition, when you understand your vet beyond the consultation room, when you start to see her being more than a vet (no one is born a vet and remains a vet only!), it will also allow you to better appreciate her and you will find out if your beliefs align or not. It is usually NOT because your beliefs differ from your vet's that mistrust occurs. Mistrust usually occurs because your vet does not know your beliefs and vice versa. After all, it is not uncommon to fear the unknown. Once you have communicated effectively and aligned your beliefs with her, an immense relief for both will occur.

Finally, this allows the approach to your pet and you to be more tailored and specific, resulting in better outcomes. It is where your goals are achieved, beliefs supported and expectations met. By doing so, you are also helping your vet to perform her job with more confidence, competence and satisfaction.

Step 4. Honesty is the Best Policy

Sometimes, unwittingly and not purposefully, hidden agendas may be carried by you or your vet.

Mary refused to accept any treatment for her pet as she was just diagnosed with cancer and did not feel that she would live long enough to take care of her pet and thus, was looking for any opportunity for euthanasia. It was only when her vet found out about her condition and addressed her concerns that treatment was able to be given to her pet leading to a full recovery. Mary was happier, relieved and satisfied in the end.

Likewise, there was a vet who kept suggesting the cheapest (not necessarily the best) treatment option to a pet guardian, Richard, because she felt he could not afford anything more and did not want to make him feel bad by suggesting other (potentially more effective) treatments that cost more. However, it was revealed that Richard would have actually paid more if he had known about the other treatments.

In both situations, the best intentions were present but the execution was flawed, leading to suboptimal results. You should maintain honesty and openness about your intentions and concerns at all times to minimise assumptions, presumptions and ill-informed decisions resulting in not-as-ideal outcomes. To do so relies on mutual trust.

Step 5. Tell Me What to Expect!

It can be a challenge for you to manage your vet's expectations. It may sound weird that her expectations need to be managed considering you are the paying customer and presumably, should get what you want. However, the expectations for the well-being for your pet can vary greatly, making it a challenge for your vet. For example, your vet may have certain presumptions leading to expected outcomes like expecting you to be able to clean a wound three times daily and you struggle to do so because of work commitments. If your vet does not know that you are not able to do so, the expected recovery may differ from reality. If your vet is aware of your limitations, she will be able to suggest another suitable treatment plan.

On the other hand, if your vet failed to manage your expectations, you would not be pleased. For example, for a tumour removal that required a wide margin (a large portion of 'normal' skin around the tumour to be removed as well), if you are not warned of the size of the surgical area, your reactions on seeing your pet after the surgery may range from mildly surprised to absolute total shock. It could even possibly lead to you regretting consenting to the surgery. When communication is poor before the surgery and your expectations were not managed, even though all tumour was successfully removed with no chance of regrowth (problem sorted), you may be unhappy and shocked at the unexpected surgical site. Success is not entirely complete.

Managing your expectations from the start could have prevented your stress and unhappiness. It is usually when expectations fall short of reality that dissatisfaction occurs. Communication is key.

- **The cost of not having a great relationship with your vet**

  It may sound excessive and a lot of hard work for you to build a relationship with your vet. It may be so, but consider the alternative.

  If your relationship with your vet was purely transactional, when your pet is healthy, you get stressed at any hint of illness for it means going to your vet who you are not familiar with and presents a lot of unknowns (stress involved). When your pet is ill and under the care of your vet, more unknowns causing stress spring up as now expectations and finances need to be managed.

Although you do not usually strive to go to your vet unless your pet is ill, when you do go, it can be quite stressful. Why not increase the amount of relief and trust by investing in your relationship with your vet at the beginning BEFORE you need her services?

Takeaway: In this chapter, you have learnt the importance of a successful relationship with your vet. You have seen the different desirable attributes of your vet and you. You have also discovered some tips that would assist in forming this meaningful partnership. Not only would your pet benefit from swift medical care when needed, both your vet and you would also thrive in this amazing rapport.

THE KEY TO ANY GREAT RELATIONSHIP IS LEARNING TO CELEBRATE THE SIMILARITIES AND RESPECTING THE DIFFERENCES.

THE END AND THE BEGINNING...

Liz loves going to the vets. She feels safe and knows that her vet understands her expectations and respects her beliefs. She has put in effort to educate her vet. As a result, it empowered her vet to help in the way she wants to be helped. Mutual trust, appreciation and respect are born and loyalty developed. Liz feels in control and in charge of her pet, even during illness when she is relying on her vet. She approaches her vet with confidence. She feels she has become her pet's hero.

You have explored how veterinary medicine is 80% human, 20% animal as it clearly has a more profound impact on you than your pet. You were reminded that it is actually more of a pet guardianship than ownership. You learnt that going to your vet need not have a negative association. As your pet's guardian, remember you are his CEO and now you have the knowledge. Your beliefs should be respected and expectations met. Your vet's mind may be trained differently but the intention is the same, to provide the best care for your pet. Delving into the finances of the veterinary profession will have given you an insight into the value of veterinary medicine. And finally, tips have been provided to make your vet work with you and for you, with pleasure in a symbiotic relationship so your pet can benefit the most.

This book was written to help you develop the best relationship you can with your vet. Your pet is important to you. He is truly a unique being and amazing individual. He shares something in common with you because you are special, and deserves the best too. Now you have the knowledge and power to obtain the most out of your vet and build a cool relationship. The results may surprise you.

Remember, your vet wants to do a great job. Help your vet to help you. She will thank you for it!

This is the End of the book and the Beginning of Your Journey. You and your pet's future depends on the steps you take now. These are three suggested steps for you to START NOW.

1. Make an appointment with your vet to discuss your beliefs and expectations, using the information you have received in this book. Be sure to discuss your financial expectations regardless of whether your pet is insured or not.

2. Your vet may not be receptive. Don't give up. Have patience and faith. Remember how you and your pet will benefit from this.

3. If you are hitting a brick wall, you may wish to consider looking for a new vet as disappointment may ensue in future anyway.

Knowledge is not power. Applied Knowledge is Power. Take action NOW.

If you like to receive more tips about Pet Guardianship or veterinary medicine, SUBSCRIBE NOW to 'Dr Lennon at Amity' on YouTube and join us on Facebook 'Is my Vet for Real?'

Did this book help you in some way? If so, I'd love to hear about it. Honest reviews help readers find the right book for their needs. Please leave a review on Amazon. When your review is LIVE, please email ismyvetforreal@gmail.com to receive an exclusive, high-quality PDF of 'Six Devastating Facts about Pet Insurance' as a token of appreciation. *Thank you.*

If you need any further assistance in your guardianship journey or have any feedback (which will be greatly appreciated) for this book, please email ismyvetforreal@gmail.com.

BONUS 1

This is almost guaranteed to work EVERY TIME to make your vet salivate and remember you as an AMAZING Pet Guardian (even if you do NOT have a pet!).

This is a secret that some Pet Guardians know and have used it to their extreme advantage, and have received 'special' VIP treatment because of it! Read more to find out how...

Vets are extremely strange creatures. Some gain satisfaction through making animals better. Others enjoy being great at honing their skill. Several savour gratitude from the pet guardians, in verbal form (saying 'thank you'), reviews or hand-written letters.

OK, this is the strange thing. In my experience working with over 100 vets and vet nurses, the pet guardians that are the most memorable and made the strongest impact are those who brought food to them. Yes, the pet guardians who showed great commitment, had been through horrendous times with their pets and survived to tell the tale, or very appreciative customers were all remembered fondly. However, it was those who filled the vets' and nurses' guts and satisfied their palates that got the most mentions!

It is truly weird. I remember vets and nurses recalling pet guardians that had not really had too much of a memorable experience (in terms of treating their pet) but gave them some form of food. Those pet guardians were very well remembered! It could be biscuits, chocolate, bread, fruits or any other form of delicacy. They seemed to be remembered more from giving food than saying 'thank you' (no matter how profusely), writing cards, awarding reviews or even recommending new customers!

It seems like the way to woo vets and nurses is through their bellies! There may be many vets and nurses that would disagree with me. Surely, they are not so shallow! Still, I would challenge you to present your vet team with some form of food and observe their response. You get MASSIVE bonus points if you do a bit of research into their preferences. For example, present their favourite food (chocolate, cake, biscuits are winners!) or know about their allergies and give them food accordingly (like gluten free or vegan). Do this and see (and feel) the difference.

It works even if you are a 'nightmare' pet guardian. It never ceases to amaze me how much vets and nurses will put up with as long as food is provided. I know of an extremely demanding (almost unreasonable) client who on multiple occasions would make unreasonable requests but is often fondly spoken of just because she brings in fresh home-made cake (her hobby) each time she comes in! I have a faint suspicion that she may not be as welcomed without her cakes!

Work experience students can benefit from this trick too! It is astounding how they are remembered better if they brought some form of edible treat for the team at the end of their placement. They are remembered more fondly than others who may have been better workers! It is really strange but true.

As bizarre as it may sound, the amount of goodwill generated is almost in direct proportion to the amount of food you bring to your vet. I have seen practice owners giving discounts off the vet bill in amounts more than the cost of the food supplied by the pet guardian to the vets and nurses. How the economics works is beyond me. I know it works as I have done similar as well! It seems that the positive value created is more than the cost of the food.

There you go, a trade secret and an extremely simple way to foster goodwill with your vet! Do not take my word but challenge it by putting it to the test! Please let me know the results you get by emailing ismyvetforreal@gmail.com. I look forward to hearing from you!

BONUS 2

Top 10 Tips to Save Money at

Your Vets

One BIG reason you may hate going to the vets is because it costs £££. The reality is that pets do cost money, the question is how much? Below are my Top 10 Tips to Save Money at Your Vets. Your vet may even thank you for following them!

1. Let's see the Vet…. AGAIN! – The Usefulness of Regular Vet Visits

   Regular visits to your vet may not only be cost saving but also life changing. Your pet's weight can be monitored to ensure it is appropriate. Early dental advice may be given. Growing lumps can be examined. I would recommend at least a visit every six months. If your pet is elderly (> 8 years old for dog and >10 years old for cat), I would recommend to see your vet every 3-4 months for a health visit.

Even if you choose not vaccinate your pet, regular vet visits are still relevant and advisable, not dissimilar to having regular dental check-ups.

"BIG PROBLEMS BECOME LITTLE PROBLEMS. LITTLE PROBLEMS BECOME NO PROBLEM."

– Chinese saying

2.   Other People's Money - Pet Insurance

It is not unusual for living things to fall ill, just like us. It is not common knowledge how much veterinary bills can be. Whereas pet insurance does not buy health, it does buy peace of mind that when your pet is ill, the choice of best treatment would not be due to the cost.

If you have used pet insurance in the past, you would usually find it invaluable. And if you have not, you may feel it is a waste of money. Unfortunately, when your pet falls ill, you may have to choose treatment options based on affordability.

Be sure to choose your policy very carefully as many may be inappropriate. Your vet may help you with it.

3. Health is Wealth – The Rewards of Boring Maintenance

Proper husbandry can help reduce many health conditions. Feeding the right amount of a good quality food can ensure great health. Making sure your pet is of appropriate body condition, not overweight or underweight, can greatly reduce the risk of many conditions like diabetes, arthritis and malnourishment.

Brushing his teeth (not the easiest for some, especially cats!) may reduce the need for dental treatment. Your vet may be able to give you some tips for doing so.

Keeping the claws trimmed can prevent ingrown claws that are excessively long. If you are not able to trim your pet's claws yourself, it is always worth having regular visits to your vet to make sure they are short to prevent unwanted bills associated with trauma, inflammation and/or infection. Also, your pet will stay pain free and thank you for it!

There may not be sex appeal to this tip but it works! It would be worth having a chat with your vet to find out things you can do to keep your pet healthy.

4. Stop-This-Train-I-Wanna-Get-Off Medicine

Preventative medicine can be controversial if seen as 'over-treatment' as treatment is administered without symptoms. This is not meant to be a debate to discuss if it is right or wrong.

However, there are certain conditions that can easily be prevented. Flea infestations are fairly common in dogs and cats. You would prefer not to have extra pets! It may also lead to skin diseases due to the fleas feeding and/or the pets scratching. So, prevention of fleas is preferable. Tick-borne diseases can cause your pet to be quite ill. Hence, its prevention is also warranted.

Pyometras (infected wombs) and unwanted pregnancies are not uncommon and can be prevented by spaying dogs and cats. Veterinary intervention for pyometras and pregnancies (if a Caesarean-section or other medical conditions relating to pregnancies is needed) may result in unexpected veterinary bills which may be substantial.

There are certain conditions like distemper, parvo, hepatitis and leptospirosis that can be life threatening and fatal. Vaccination can prevent or greatly reduce the chance of contracting these viruses and bacteria.

Please do discuss with your vet what would be appropriate for your pet in terms of preventative medicine.

5. Know Your Pet, Know Thyself

    Having knowledge and understanding of your pet may help you to know when to call the vet and not leave it too late. Be familiar with your pet's daily habits like how much he drinks and eats, the normal behaviour, his habits, quirks, personality, his defecation habits, what is normal and abnormal for him.

    The more you understand your pet, the more you will know when something is wrong. If you are very 'tuned in' with your pet, usually, you will be able to tell something is wrong even if your vet cannot see it. If you feel you know your pet well, trust your gut, you are usually correct.

6. Your Vet, Your Choice

    Choosing your vet may be the most important thing you can do in terms of taking care of your pet's medical health and your own sanity. It can be easy to look for the cheapest vet around and usually, you will get what you pay for. Sometimes, the result may be more costly than what you pay for and I am not referring to money. Cheap is expensive.

    Focus on the value you will receive rather than the cost of what you would pay. Value may not always involve money. Peace of mind, trust and faith cannot be measured by money but they are priceless. Look for a vet that provides you with those attributes and it may be money well spent. Find a vet you can trust that suits your expectations, "style" and budget. What you pay is cost and what you receive is value.

7. Savings in Black and White — Ask for Written Prescriptions

Medicines obtained via internet pharmacies are usually considerably much more cost effective compared to getting them from your vets. It is usually due to the differences in overheads and economy of scale (they can buy medicine at bulk quantities that has a larger discount).

If your vet is willing, don't be afraid to request a prescription that may allow you to make a saving.

Few points to note — 1. The prescription will be written for the length of time that your vet determines is appropriate before the next medical check-up. 2. There are no guarantees that the drug you receive will be authentic (there have been a lot of fake internet pharmacies providing medications of dubious origin and quality). 3. There would be an appropriate charge for your vet writing the prescription. Prescriptions are not free!

This may be more useful for long-term medications.

8.   Help-I-have-NO-MONEY-at-all Treatment - PDSA

People's Dispensary for Sick Animals (PDSA) is a UK-based charity providing veterinary care for pet guardians who are on benefits and/or are in financial difficulties. It is usually extremely low cost or free in some circumstances. You will have to check your eligibility and find out where your closest PDSA vet practice is (you can do both online). As it is a budget practice, not all treatment options will be made available but at least your pet gets treated.

9.   Let's Talk about MONEY, baby!

If you truly want to save money at the vets, it would make sense to speak to your vet about it. Discuss your financial expectations with her. Make it clear what you expect and what you can afford. With that knowledge, she can further advise you what to expect with that budget. If you were to buy a car from a garage, you would tell the salesman your budget so he would give you the appropriate selection of car. He would not be selling a Rolls Royce on a Ford budget. Similarly, help your vet to help you by providing her with your expectations. Most people do not like to talk about money but money is all that is talked about at the end. Why not take the plunge and discuss it FIRST so it needs not to be discussed awkwardly later?

Also, remember that pets do cost money. Before you get a pet, factor that in and be sure to have the means to take care of him in health and in sickness. If you are not going to take out insurance, be sure to put aside a budget for him. Like the Scout motto, "Be Prepared!"

10. A Stitch in Time Saves Nine – Practice Safety First!

While it is impossible to avoid accidents in life, it is possible to practice basic home and environment safety for your pet.

Be aware of where your pets have access to. Make sure there are no live wires or anything that can cause choking or a gastro-intestinal obstruction that they can chew or swallow. Be sure to keep all human medication or potential poisons out of reach.

If you live in a multi-storey house, make sure your kitten is safe from falling out of the window. Throwing sticks can cause them to be stuck in the mouth or throat. Trapping pets' tails in doors (especially conservatory doors!) and windows can be prevented.

Being aware of where your pets are around your (or your children's) feet and not stepping on them helps! Teaching young children how to approach and play with your pet is invaluable, both in reducing injuries to both parties and maximising their relationship.

Attending a dog first-aid course may be a great investment and invaluable during times of need.

Summary

Money worries can be one of the greatest headaches as your pet's guardian. It can also destroy great relationships. Taking a proactive lead in identifying and eliminating these worries can lead to peace of mind, satisfaction and happiness to enable the most fulfilling relationship with your pet (and your vet!). Be Conscious, Be Aware and Take the Lead!

N.B. This list is not exhaustive and if you feel you have more to add, please email ismyvetforreal@gmail.com.

We will be grateful for any further contributions!

BONUS 3

Things that only make sense when a vet says it. WARNING: You WILL LAUGH TILL YOUR SIDES HURT!

So, there are statements or questions that would sound weird, bizarre or simply rude when taken out of context. These are some examples that the veterinary profession encounter, some often, others not so often.

WARNING: DO NOT READ IF YOU ARE EASILY OFFENDED OR HAVE A WEAK STOMACH. NO ANIMALS WERE HARMED DURING THE PRODUCTION.

On Clinical Examination...

Sorry, my elbow is practically in your vagina.

Did I just knee you in your arse?

Yeah, I'll just stand there holding on to his testicles.

Please let me in your bum.

My hands are very lubey 'cos I stuck them in the vet's drawer.

Oh my god, just give me your tongue!

I'm glad I don't have a fluffy bum.

Personally, I don't like sniffing random parts of anatomy.

Sing Happy Birthday to him... it may make him have a wee, it works for me!

Ugh... I am jealous of your pelvic floor.

Shall we do some drugs?

A crusty hole is never good.

Sorry if I touched your boob... (Reply) Don't worry, it's been a while...

Are we going to stop talking about his penis yet?

She puts her head in between her legs when she doesn't want to be touched!

Ooh, someone come smell this sick! He definitely ate chocolate orange! Aw... now I want chocolate orange.

Can you please let the next appointment now I will be a little late? I just have to hold his penis.

During Surgery...

Can I have a new forcep? I touched myself with this one so it is dirty.

Don't come in prep, the vet is only wearing a bra.

Please put your penis away.

Are you talking to me or the cervix?

That's so gross, let me take a picture.

Sorry about that blood. I dropped the ball... literally.

His testicles look like chewy raisins.

After Surgery...

Can you sniff around my stomach and just check I got all the cat pee out?

Mate, have I got sh*t on my tits? Have I got sh*tty titties?

I'm covered in literally every bodily fluid ever and the worst part is, I have to change into pink scrubs and that is just not my colour.

I would rather have dry hands than placenta-covered hands.

When dealing with a Pyometra (pus-filled infected womb)...

The colour of that pyo makes a lovely lipstick colour.

If I get pyo anywhere near my vagina, I will be so mad!

It's my birthday, I am popping the pyo!

On Reflections...

Aw, look at his man bag... oh, it's a cat!

How are you this far into your career and never sniffed

a paw?!

Actually, he has quite a large bum hole.

There's nothing wrong with putting a finger up there.

Imagine having a dangly vulva.

Do I smell like ears? Wait, I smell like ears, don't I?

Does my boob smell like arse to you?

His feet don't smell nice, that is such a shame.

This dog's bum is so comfy... and it smells really good too!

APPENDIX

https://www.statista.com/statistics/308218/leading-ten-pets-ranked-by-household-ownership-in-the-united-kingdom-uk/

https://www.vettimes.co.uk/news/37-of-survey-respondents-seek-to-leave-vet-profession/

Why are vets at high risk of suicide?

https://veterinaryrecord.bmj.com/content/164/19/575

https://www.pdsa.org.uk/taking-care-of-your-pet/looking-after-your-pet/puppies-dogs/the-cost-of-owning-a-dog

https://consumer.healthday.com/encyclopedia/stress-management-37/stress-health-news-640/pets-and-stress-646064.html

https://www.health.harvard.edu/staying-healthy/having-a-dog-can-help-your-heart--literally

Having a cat can reduce stroke risk

https://www.medicalnewstoday.com/articles/98432#1

https://www.ncbi.nlm.nih.gov/pmc/articles/PMC33173

29/

https://can-do-canines.org/our-dogs/ourdogs/diabetes-assist-dogs/

https://www.diabetes.co.uk/hypo-alert-dogs.html

Having a pet reduces allergies in their guardians
https://www.ncbi.nlm.nih.gov/pmc/articles/PMC2783630/

Non-verbal communication
https://ubiquity.acm.org/article.cfm?id=2043156

RVC Number One College in the World
https://london.ac.uk/ways-study/study-campus-london/member-institutions/royal-veterinary-college

Pet insurance in Sweden
https://news.vin.com/default.aspx?pid=210&Id=9305364&useobjecttypeid=10&fromVINNEWSASPX=1

Lawyer's Salary
https://www.lawsociety.org.uk/law-careers/becoming-a-solicitor/how-much-do-solicitors-earn/

https://www.lex100.com/survey/how-much-will-you-earn-as-a-trainee-and-newly-qualified-solicitor/

https://www.chambersstudent.co.uk/where-to-

start/newsletter/how-much-do-trainee-lawyers-earn
https://www.prospects.ac.uk/jobs-and-work-experience/job-sectors/law-sector/how-much-do-lawyers-earn

Accountant's Salary
https://www.accountancyage.com/2018/04/18/salary-survey-2018-uk-accountants-earning-right-now/

Doctor's Salary
https://www.bma.org.uk/pay-and-contracts/pay/junior-doctors-pay-scales/pay-scales-for-junior-doctors-in-england
https://www.bma.org.uk/pay-and-contracts/pay/consultants-pay-scales/pay-scales-for-consultants-in-england

Dentist's Salary
https://www.healthcareers.nhs.uk/explore-roles/dental-team/roles-dental-team/dentist/pay-dentists
https://www.cv-library.co.uk/salary-guide/average-dentist-salary.

ABOUT THE AUTHOR

Dr Lennon Foo GPCert(SAM) MRCVS founded Amity Vets whose core purpose is Empowering You Through Education. Despite veterinary medicine being extremely scientific, he believes it should extend further than merely treating animals. He believes it should include and embrace the unique beauty of the bond between your pet and you.

Dr Lennon Foo is a practising vet for 15 years. He has an advanced certificate in Small Animal Medicine and loves surgery. He is especially interested in acupuncture, keyhole surgery and exotic pets.

Working in various countries including Thailand, Spain, Egypt and Greece on multiple occasions for charity projects either training local vets or providing veterinary care and guiding policy, Lennon has worked with over ten thousand pet guardians, performed over 60,000 consultations and had more than 90,000 pet guardian interactions. He is also a well-established public speaker and runs a YouTube channel (Dr Lennon Foo at Amity), providing tips for you to understand more about your pets and the veterinary profession.

Salsa dancing, roller skating and capoeira make up his non veterinary pursuits.

He lives in Devon, UK with his family.

Find out more about Lennon at www.drlennonfoo.com

Amity Veterinary Care

At Amity, you are empowered through education turning you into your pet's hero. You are recognized as a sacred individual who have taken up the courage and brave responsibility of being your pet's guardian. Their aim is to help your pet and you win.

You can rest assure that you and your pet will be taken care of. You will have peace of mind that your veterinary needs are met with compassion and empathy. You will also learn more about your pet.

Amity is UK's first and only members practice. This enables the right services to be provided for the right guardians to achieve the right results. By joining us, you will become part of an exclusive group of pet guardians who treat their pets like family with dedicated personalised veterinary care.

It has a free YouTube channel (Dr Lennon at Amity) that is dedicated to provide information to empower your knowledge on your pet and the veterinary profession. Be sure to subscribe to it to receive simple, effective and extremely useful content.

Please visit www.amityvets.co.uk

or email ismyvetforreal@gmail.com for more information.

Printed in Great Britain
by Amazon

58877536R00139